Horror and Mystery Photoplay Editions
and Magazine Fictionizations

TWO NEW FILMS IN COMPLETE STORY FORM FOR 2d.

SCREEN Stories 2ᴰ

No. 143.　　　　Twopence—Every Wednesday.　　　　October 29th, 1932.

A Strange & Dismal House and the Evil Spectre that lived behind its walls.

A GRIPPING MYSTERY DRAMA —

"The THIRTEENTH GUEST"

Horror and Mystery Photoplay Editions and Magazine Fictionizations

The Catalog of a Collection

Thomas Mann

McFarland & Company, Inc., Publishers
Jefferson, North Carolina, and London

Dedicated to film enthusiasts and book collectors
who share a fondness for these old stories

**Frontispiece: Cover of *Screen Stories* showing a scene
from *The Thirteenth Guest*.**

LIBRARY OF CONGRESS CATALOGUING-IN-PUBLICATION DATA

Mann, Thomas, 1948–
    Horror and mystery photoplay editions and magazine
fictionizations : the catalog of a collection / Thomas Mann.
       p.   cm.
    Includes bibliographical references and index.

    ISBN 0-7864-1722-6 (softcover : 50# alkaline paper)

    1. Photoplay editions—Bibliography.   2. Film
novelizations—Bibliography.   3. Horror films.
4. Detective and mystery films. I. Title.
Z5917.P48M36   2004
[PN3435]
016.80883'8738—dc22   2004001525

British Library cataloguing data are available

Manufactured in the United States of America

Cover illustration from the dust jacket of the 1928 photoplay
of *The Terror* by Edgar Wallace

McFarland & Company, Inc., Publishers
  Box 611, Jefferson, North Carolina 28640
    www.mcfarlandpub.com

Table of Contents

The Readers Library Film Edition has been instituted to meet a real modern demand. Interest in a film is by no means exhausted merely by seeing it. The two arts, or forms of expression, the picture and the written word in book form, react one on the other. Imagination, stimulated by the film, is yet not satisfied until its story is wholly absorbed. In a word, the filmgoer wishes also to read the book of the film, and the reader to see the picture.

[Foreword to *The Girl in The Moon*]

"My library fire never looked so alluring as on that night. Also, I was engaged in some very entertaining researches."
"I beg your pardon?" said Billy Magee.
"Some very entertaining research work."
"Yes," reflected Magee slowly, "I suppose such things do exist. Go on, please."

[*Seven Keys to Baldpate*]

Preface

Photoplay editions, sometimes called movie editions, were inexpensive hardcover books published from the 1910s through the 1940s. They were reprints of novels that had just been made into movies, illustrated with bound-in photographs of scenes from the films. Sometimes the photos appeared at intervals throughout the book, sometimes on the endpapers; at times, especially in the 1940s, they appeared only on the dust jacket. Although in most cases the films were based on prior novels, occasionally the movies came first and the novelizations were created from the film scripts, as with the Pearl White serial *The Perils of Pauline*, or the Lon Chaney silent *London After Midnight*. These books filled the niche taken up by the paperback "movie tie-in" editions of today; this is the terminology that became more prevalent from the 1950s onward, by which time the term "photoplay" had taken on almost antiquarian connotations. None of these volumes have any connection with *Photoplay Magazine*, which most people think of when they hear the term.

The present volume is a catalog of an unusually large collection, assembled over four decades, of photoplay editions and magazine-story fictionizations tied to old horror movies and mysteries. Some books not strictly in these fields are included if they are linked to films made by stars such as Lon Chaney, Boris Karloff, Bela Lugosi, and other genre performers. Mysteries are generally understood to feature a detective as the central character, rather than simply to have a crime as a plot element. Some *film noir* books, and some associated with Alfred Hitchcock films, are also included. Adventure or fantasy stories having an *outré* element are considered within scope, as are science fiction titles. With a few exceptions, the cut-off point for inclusion is the year 1970. In any such collection the edges will necessarily be somewhat blurred; in this case I can do no better than to quote the famous comment of U.S. Supreme Court Justice Potter Stewart, who remarked regarding pornography, "I shall not today attempt further to define the kinds of material ... But I know it when I see it."

Other related bibliographies exist, but the present volume comple-
ments them in significant ways. The most comprehensive bibliography
of all photoplay books, not limited by genre, is Arnie Davis's *Photoplay
Editions and Other Movie Tie-In Books: The Golden Years 1912-1969* (East
Waterboro, Maine: Mainely Books, 2002). This list includes American
and foreign imprints in the English language, hardcovers and paperbacks,
and adult and juvenile titles from 1912 through 1969. It is particularly rich
in providing 1,132 photo reproductions, many in color, of covers and dust
jacket illustrations. Moe Wadle's *The Movie Tie-In Book* (Coralville, Iowa:
Nostalgia Books, 1994) is an excellent list of American paperback movie
editions published from 1939 to 1980. Rick Miller's *Photoplay Editions: A
Collector's Guide* (Jefferson, North Carolina: McFarland, 2002) is a listing of American and foreign books in English, excluding paperbacks and
juvenile titles; it also includes citations to sixty stage play editions (books
illustrated with scenes from stage productions rather than films). Unlike
the Davis book, it includes extensive indexes. Like the others, however,
Miller's list is not limited by genre—that is, it lists not only tie-ins to
horror films and mysteries, but westerns, melodramas, war stories,
romances, comedies, and so on. Another useful bibliography is devoted
exclusively to titles published by The Readers Library Publishing Co.,
Ltd., in London, the preeminent source of British photoplay editions; it
is Richard Williams's *Readers Library* (British Hardback Checklists:
Number One [ISBN 1 871122 15 5]. Second Edition, Revised, January
2000. The Dragonby Press, 15 High Street, Dragonby, Scunthorpe, North
Lincolnshire, DN15 0BE, England). The above titles supersede an older,
pioneering work in this area of bibliography, Emil Petaja's *Photoplay Edition* (San Francisco, California: SISU Publishers, 1975).

The present volume overlaps with these bibliographies in its cover-
age of books, but considerably extends the field beyond books to fictionizations (within horror and mystery genres) in the format of movie-magazine
novelizations and, to a lesser extent, comic books and Big Little Books.
(The term "fictionized," rather than "fictionalized," is used regularly in
the items themselves.) Stage play tie-ins, omitted by Davis and minimally
covered by Miller, are also included. Fuller annotations of book titles, too,
may be found here. Another difference lies in the fact that this is not a
bibliography of all possible titles, but a catalog of a particular collection,
albeit a very large one; and so peculiarities of some of its individual physical volumes will be noted. I hope, however, that the way in which this
is done will lead other collectors to look again at their own volumes in
perhaps new ways, and with greater enjoyment.

As noted, the cut-off date for inclusion in this list is generally 1970. A few exceptions have been made in order to include tie-ins to later films of prominent genre figures such as stop-motion animator Ray Harryhausen or actor Peter Cushing. The choice of that year is not entirely arbitrary. The scary movies of the 1960s that I enjoyed so much as an adolescent and that awakened my collecting interest—both those showing in the theaters and the older, classic films that appeared regularly on television—were quite different from the type that became the norm in the early 1970s and afterward. The ones I grew to enjoy featured monsters or frightening elements, of course, but they were always in a moral universe where "the forces of good" won at the end of the movie. Dracula or Frankenstein's monster might readily (and very ingeniously) be revived somehow in a sequel; but at the end of any given movie, the viewer could reasonably believe that they'd been completely vanquished.

The "givenness" of that expectation changed with *Night of the Living Dead* in 1968, an unfortunately too-influential film that altered the conventions of most subsequent horror movies. It led to a regridding of the whole genre into a cynical, even nihilistic worldview in which the forces of evil or chaos tend to triumph at the end of films. Slasher and *Chainsaw Massacre* movies, substituting "splatter" and explicit gore in place of shadows, suggestion, and atmosphere, soon followed, further reframing and degrading the fundamental orientation of the entire genre. Exceptions exist, of course, but the period around 1970 remains a watershed.

The present catalog, then, in focusing on the pre–1970 era, is intended to serve not just as a reference work but as a tribute, and not just to the films but to the novels and short fictionizations of that more innocent period.

Thomas Mann, March 2004

Introduction

There are as many reasons to collect books as there are collectors. In retrospect, I can see that one prominent motivation behind my own initial efforts lay in the peculiarities of the film environment of the 1960s, when I began collecting. At that time I usually assumed I would never get to actually see most of the old movies to which photoplay books were linked, and that the volumes themselves were as close a substitute as I would ever find. This, after all, was a period well before videos, DVDs, and cable TV, in which fans of Golden Age movies were almost entirely at the mercy of local television stations, or of a very few repertory film houses.

The proliferation of the newer means of access to older films was and is a most welcome development. I have found, however, that many of the films fictionized in the collection, which I thought at the time were simply inaccessible to a teenager in Chicago, are now in fact considered entirely "lost" to everyone, and the photo-illustrated book or magazine novelizations of them that remain are indeed likely to continue being our closest means of approximating the experience of their stories. Indeed, an important inducement to continue collecting, even now, is that the assumed ephemerality of these popular novels and magazines has usually led conventional libraries to neglect them; and so, as is often the case in literary and film history, private collectors can serve an important role in preserving material whose significance to cultural studies becomes apparent to institutions only in retrospect.

Two examples of "lost" films being preserved, in a sense, through fictionized counterparts are *A Blind Bargain* and *The Gorilla*. The former was a 1922 Goldwyn horror melodrama featuring Lon Chaney in a dual role as a mad doctor and his animal-like assistant (the result of an experiment gone wrong). The film has been lovingly reconstructed in book form, with the same title, by Philip J. Riley (Atlantic City, N.J.: MagicImage Filmbooks, 1988), using contemporary stills, promotional material, and script elements from a number of archival sources, both public and private. The volume is a real feast for genre fans. As elaborate a reconstruction as it is, however, it overlooks the existence of an obscure short story fictionization of the film, with photos, published in the magazine *Moving Picture Stories* in 1923 (the full citation appears in the present volume).

The Gorilla, based on a play by Ralph Spence, was originally filmed in 1927 by First National; among its cast members was a youthful Walter Pidgeon. It is an "old house thriller" of a genre very popular in the 1920s and 1930s, including such other titles as *The Bat* and *The Cat and the Canary*. One hesitates to say that the film is entirely lost, since surprising footage still turns up occasionally in garages, Czech archives, and even frozen swimming pools in Alaska; still, the current consensus is that this film is indeed among the missing. And yet, it too "survives" in a tie-in short story version, with photos, in another issue of *Moving Picture Stories*. "The Gorilla," having now fallen into the public domain, is reproduced in this book; I think it captures well something of the flavor of these spooky old tie-in stories.

Some of the photoplay books that are novelizations of their respective films sometimes also "preserve"—with a minimal suspension of disbelief—individual scenes that are now lost from the otherwise-surviving movies. For any collector of photoplays, the example that springs immediately to mind is that of the "censored spider pit scene" from *King Kong*. The sequence, as originally filmed by master stop-motion animator Willis O'Brien, showed the giant gorilla shaking a group of helpless sailors off a log bridge into a ravine in which they were swarmed upon by horrible predatory creatures, including a giant spider. The scene was deleted by one of the film's producers because its gruesome details formed too great a parenthesis in the pacing of the film's action; its footage is now thought to be permanently lost. The sequence missing from the movie, however, is not missing from the contemporary photoplay novelization by Delos W. Lovelace:

> As though exorcised by his pointing figure, a spider like a keg on many legs came crawling out of a cave. It may not have been aware of the watchers on the high margin of the ravine, but every one would have sworn the thing stared up malevolently. Something which would have been a lizard except for its size lay warming itself on a sunny ledge. The spider moved toward it, then thought better of the impulse and looked about for smaller prey. This was provided by a round, crawling object with tentacles like those of an octopus. The spider crawled to the attack. Both octopus-insect and spider vanished into a fissure.

"I'm not going to cross that log with those things under me," a
sailor announced.

* * *

Two of the men lost their holds. One grasped madly at the face
of a prone comrade and left bloody finger marks as he went
whirling down into the decaying silt at the bottom. He had no
more than struck when the lizard flashed upon him. Driscoll,
watching, hoped that the complete lack of movement meant uncon-
sciousness, or, better, that death had come immediately. The second
man did not die in the fall. He was not even unconscious. He
landed feet first, sinking immediately to his waistline in the mud,
and screamed horribly as not one but half a dozen of the great spiders swarmed over him.

Up on the edge of the ravine the triceratop stamped the ground.
Getting no notice from his adversary across the gap he bellowed
uncertainly and began backing up. With a last bellow he wheeled
around and lumbered toward the trees.

Kong lifted the log and jerked it again. Another man fell, prey
for a new outpouring of spiders. Another jerk, and the octopus-
insect, along with a score of companions, began to fight against the
spiders and the lizards for the booty. Only one man was left on the
log and he clung desperately. Kong jerked, but could not shake him
loose. Nor could all the despairing efforts of Driscoll and Denham,
all their shouts, all their rocks, turn the beast-god from his purpose.
The clinging man shrieked. Kong glowered down upon him and in
a culminating exasperation swung the log far sideways and dropped
it. The end caught on the very edge of the ravine and then slipped
slowly off to drop like a battering ram upon the insects at their
feast below.

Discoveries such as this, especially in a period prior to paperback
reprints of the obscure original photoplay hardcover, served as the lure
to motivate many a weekend expedition to out-of-the-way secondhand
bookstores. (By the way, a *King Kong* edition in its original dustjacket,
while not the rarest of film tie-in books, is often now considered by collectors and dealers to be the most desirable of all photoplay titles.)

The area of collecting magazine fictionizations of film stories, such
as those for *A Blind Bargain* or *The Gorilla*, is a relatively new field for
collectors; it has opened in recent years only because of the Internet.
No comprehensive bibliography of magazine-story film adaptations has
been compiled because of the difficulty of finding complete runs of the
relevant magazines, which were generally considered too insubstantial
for institutional libraries to collect and preserve. The appearance of
"attic" material for sale on Internet, however, in sites such as eBay,
bookfinder.com, and addall.com—and in some other sites now defunct—

has finally provided an avenue of access to large, if unsystematic, groups of these old magazines, often indexed at the level of their tables of contents. I hope the present listing of these stories will serve as a baseline for further compilations, somewhat in the way that Emil Petaja's original bibliography of photoplay books, based on his own collection, pioneered bibliographical efforts in that area.

What is particularly enjoyable about the magazine stories is that they fill one of the definite gaps in the field, of which collectors have long been aware. One such gap, for many years, was the lack of comprehensive bibliographies that would alert searchers to titles whose existence is not revealed through simple bookstore or Internet browsing. This hole has now been admirably filled by the Davis, Miller, Wadle, and Williams bibliographies mentioned earlier, which now supersede the pioneering (but very incomplete) list by Petaja.

Another remaining gap in the field is the simple fact that many Golden Age horror movies and mysteries that seemingly *ought* to have generated tie-in photoplay editions just never did. *The Mummy* (1932), for example, cried out for a contemporary novelization, given the popularity of Boris Karloff at the time, and given his appearances in other contemporary photoplay editions such as *Frankenstein* and *The Old Dark House*. Similarly, *The Raven*, which united Karloff and Bela Lugosi onscreen, would also have been a natural choice for a movie edition hardback, especially since the Edgar Allan Poe stories were copyright free and had already spawned a *Murders in the Rue Morgue* tie-in hardback volume with Lugosi photos. Yet neither film generated a photoplay book. What actually happened, however, is that both stories were indeed fictionized at the time and published with photos from their movie versions in contemporary film magazines. And not just these two, but hundreds of others as well—including *The Cat Creeps, The Maltese Falcon, Mad Love, Mark of the Vampire, Phantom of the Opera* (Claude Rains version), *Secret of the Blue Room, The Thin Man, The Uninvited,* and *The Werewolf of London.*

What is especially exciting for an enthusiast in this area is that some of the classic horror or mystery movies generated two (or more) different magazine novelizations: widely variant fictionizations of "The Mummy," for example, appeared in *The Mystery Magazine* and *Screen Romances* in January and February of 1933, respectively, and both were heavily illustrated with photos from the Karloff film. A third version appears in the British serial *Boy's Cinema Annual 1934,* and a fourth in another British publication, *The Film Star Weekly* of May 13, 1933. Here are the openings of all four:

"The Mummy" from *Boy's Cinema Annual 1934.*

Whenever I waver, whenever I regret my lost correspondency in the International Fellowship of Egyptologists, whenever I am tempted to recant my heresy and confess that my 1930 report on the circumstances in the case of Dr. Ardath Bey was the result of a brainstorm—then I look down at my right hand, where the thumb and forefinger were shriveled by contact with the mummy's cigarette. Then I know that the whole thing was literally and damnably true, that Whemple and Pearson and the Copt guard died of the rotting touch, that Helen Grosvenor *did* turn away the embalmer's knife with a prayer four thousand years old and that, through that winter week in Cairo, we were four living against one dead.

—*Mystery* (January 1933)

Dr. Muller, of Vienna, was spending his winter in Cairo. Dr. Muller spent most of his winters in Cairo, furthering his already profound knowledge. But this year he had a particular problem, and a patient. Perhaps among the deep strange secrets of this ancient land he might find an answer for her. Music in dance rhythm came to Dr. Muller's ears as he leaned over the parapet of the roof garden of the hotel Semiramis, looking across the city to where the thread of the Nile gleamed for a moment in late sunlight. Beyond lay the desert, and the tombs of the ancient kings. He thought of his good

friend, Sir Joseph Whemple, director of the British Museum in
Egypt, and of the things they had learned together in the land of
Egypt. Sir Joseph was admittedly one of the best excavators
England had ever turned out, yet it had been ten years since he had
gone down into the valleys where lay the great treasures of dead
Egypt. Ten years.... Muller had been with Whemple on that last
trip, had been in his hut on the night they had opened the mummy
case of Im-ho-tep, High Priest in the temple of the Sun at Karnak,
some thirty-seven hundred years gone.... Muller's eyes narrowed
speculatively, as he saw again in his mind's eye the agonized, dis-
torted face of that mummy—the face of a man who had been
buried alive—the mummy case from which the customary prayers
for the dead had been erased, condemning the man to death in this
world and the next....

—Screen Romances (February 1933)

The Awakening

Among those familiar with the ruins of Thebes, capital of ancient
Egypt, who has not heard of the scroll of Thoth, wherein were set
down, according to legend, those magic words by which the goddess Isis raised Osiris from the dead?

Who has not heard of that other sacred script on which the old
religion of the Pharoahs is based?

"O, Amon-Ra! O, God of Gods! Death is but the doorway to
new Life! We live to-day—we shall live again. In many forms shall
we return to this earth, O mighty one—"

These things were known to Sir Joseph Whemple, the famous
British archaeologist and leader of the Field Expedition of 1921,
commissioned by the British Museum to probe deep into the his-
toric dust and rocks of the once-flourishing city. They were known,
also, by Ralph Norton, the Oxford youth who was his assistant.
They were known, and *half-believed*, by Doctor Muller, Egyptologist and student of the occult sciences, who had agreed to help Sir
Joseph in his work of research.

It was night, and the three men stood in a crude hut built against
a desert ridge near which they had been excavating. The sum total
of their discoveries had been conveyed to that hut—a few broken
bits of pottery covered with hieroglyphics, a wooden box that had
yet to be inspected, and a mummified body in a sarcophagus which
had been set against the wall which Muller was even now examin-
ing.

—Boy's Cinema Annual 1934

"Well, dad, aren't you glad that you changed your mind and came
out to Egypt after all? It is a sensational find, isn't it?"

Young Frank Whemple leant across the big desk in the curator's
office which had been put at his father's disposal in the museum at
Cairo and spoke enthusiastically.

His father, Sir Joseph Whemple, the famous Egyptologist, looked up at his son affectionately from beneath his bushy white eyebrows. He was a striking looking old man with a broad, clever head and sharp, piercing grey eyes. The two men had been discussing the new exhibits, the relics from the newly discovered tomb of Princess Amen Ra. The tomb erected over three thousand years before had been discovered unrobbed and intact, and this sensational find had made history in the academic world.

Frank had been one of the heads of the expedition that had made the discovery, and his father had broken a ten year old vow never to return to Egypt in order to see for himself his son's success.

Frank was twenty-five, fair-haired, good looking and wildly enthusiastic.

—*The Film Star Weekly* (May 13, 1933)

The *Boy's Cinema* version follows the screenplay most directly, the *Screen Romances* and *Film Star Weekly* versions somewhat less so, but the *Mystery* version is a more highly crafted short story in its own right, linked to the movie but not entirely dependent on it. Reading such accounts is, in a way, a means of recapturing the thrill of seeing the classic film for the first time, as each variation brings an entirely fresh element to the experience. Indeed, even apart from the fun of bookstore searching, the satisfactions of preserving ephemeral material, and the enjoyment of simply reading entirely unfamiliar stories, the revivifying of old enthusiasms tied to experiences of the films themselves—recaptured through a new "side door" perspective—is one of the great attractions of collecting.

Magazine stories afford an opportunity of rounding up many of the classic Boris Karloff–Bela Lugosi screen pairings. There are, for example, two different versions (both dated 1935) of "The Raven," in *Romantic Movie Stories* and *Boy's Cinema*. Another pairing of the stars in "The Black Cat" is captured in *Romantic Movie Stories*; a third, "Black Friday," in a *Movie Story Magazine* of 1940; and a fourth, "You'll Find Out" in a *Screen Romances* issue of the same year. There is even a fifth pairing, in "Son of Frankenstein," captured in photo-sequence story form in a *Look Magazine* issue of 1939. (Bibliographic convention calls for stories published within magazines to be referred to in quotes, as "The Black Cat," while regular book or film titles are printed in italics, as *The Murders in the Rue Morgue*.)

A particularly interesting area of magazine collecting lies in a series of fictionizations of numerous Universal horror films of the 1940s, many of which starred Lon Chaney, Jr. None of these classic movies generated any contemporary book tie-ins at all, either hardcover or paperback, American or British. (This was probably due in part to paper shortages during the World War II years.) Nonetheless, there are movie magazine novelizations, with photos, of "The Wolf Man," "The Ghost of Frankenstein," "Frankenstein Meets the Wolf Man," "The Mummy's Ghost," "House of Dracula," "Abbott & Costello Meet Frankenstein," "Weird Woman," "Invisible Man's Revenge," and "The Mad Ghoul."

Other film series received comparable treatments. Examples include "The Thin Man" (multiple versions in different magazines), "After the Thin Man" (two versions), "Another Thin Man," "Song of the Thin Man," and "The Thin Man Goes Home." Peter Lorre's films are well represented in "Mr. Moto's Gamble," "Mr. Moto's Last Warning," and "Thank You, Mr. Moto." Bulldog Drummond stories are similarly numerous. Some of the Charlie Chan movies, too, that never generated hardcover photoplays nonetheless appear as illustrated magazine fictionizations, among them "Charlie Chan at Monte Carlo," which was Warner Oland's last film. Four of the Philo Vance movies appear as photo-accompanied magazine stories, "The Kennel Murder Case" (two versions), "The Gracie Allen Murder Case" (two versions), "The Dragon Murder Case" (two versions), and "Calling Philo Vance." The Basil Rathbone Sherlock Holmes films received similar treatment, including "The Hound of the Baskervilles," "Sherlock Holmes" (from *The Adventures of Sherlock Holmes*), "Dressed to Kill," "Sherlock Holmes and the Secret Weapon," and "Sherlock Holmes and the Voice of Terror." There are even illustrated story versions of classic Val Lewton films such as "The Cat People," "Curse of the Cat People," "I Walked with a Zombie," "The Leopard Man," and "Bedlam," the last with three photos of Boris Karloff.

Especially enjoyable are the horror-comedy or mystery-comedy stories. As previously mentioned, "Abbott & Costello Meet Frankenstein" appears in story form with a photo in one of these old periodicals, but so do other classics in this genre, including "The Ghost Breakers" (with Bob Hope) from 1940 and "Topper Returns" from 1941. Milton Berle, better known for his television work during the 1950s, also made mystery comedies in the early 1940s, and there is a "Whispering Ghosts" story tied to his 1942 film with John Carradine and Willie Best, in which Berle plays a "radio detective" (with Best as his valet), much like the Hope role in the 1940 film.

Magazine stories allow considerable additional scope for collectors of Lon Chaney photoplays: contemporary fictionizations exist for

"Quits" from 1915, "Outside the Law" from 1921, "A Blind Bargain" from 1922, and "Laugh, Clown, Laugh" from 1928. "Outside the Law," in its magazine version, is quite different from the film's story as novelized in the contemporaneous Jacobsen-Hodgkinson paperback version; like *Treasure Island*, it is another film in which Chaney played two different roles. "A Blind Bargain" provides yet another narrative illustrated with photos of Chaney in two makeups. In genre terms it is particularly interesting because in this story he plays both a mad doctor and his own hunchbacked assistant, nine years before *Frankenstein*. Yet another old magazine provides a tie-in to one of Chaney's most famous roles, in *The Hunchback of Notre Dame*. This film is recounted in short-story form in *The Motion Picture Magazine* of 1923—with seven photos, three more than appear in either the A. L. Burt book version of Victor Hugo's novel, or the much rarer Swarz volume that is a novel-length fictionization of the film script. These old magazines are just as scarce as the fragile newsprint paperbacks that exist for several other Chaney titles, *The Mocking Bird, Outside the Law, The Road to Mandalay, Tell It to the Marines*, and *Where East Is East*.

Let me add here that among Lon Chaney *book* tie-ins, two editions of *Treasure Island* are particularly noteworthy. The first, published by the Charles Renard Company in New York in 1925, not only shows photos of Chaney in two different pirate makeups; it also shows actors Charles Ogle and Bull Montana as other pirates. Ogle was the first actor to play the Frankenstein monster on film, in a 1910 Edison version; and Montana is "famous"—at least within the small world of genre enthusiasts—for playing the apeman in the 1925 silent version of *The Lost World*. None of these actors' names are listed on the photographs in the book itself, which are captioned only with names of the fictional characters being portrayed, but the actors playing those parts can be easily identified through the *American Film Institute Catalog*. Having identified which actors are wearing which costumes in the Renard edition, one can then spot Chaney and Montana in the same costumes within an uncaptioned group photo in an entirely different edition of *Treasure Island*, published by the Copp Clark Company in Toronto in 1926.

For many bibliophiles in this field the primary thrill of collecting lies simply in the pleasure of bringing together the books as physical objects—of discovering relevant titles and securing them either through painstaking bookstore hunts or, increasingly, via skillful Internet searches—and then, as one collector colleague put it, "holding them in

Above: Bull Montana from the Renard edition of *Treasure Island. Opposite top:* Lon Chaney (fourth adult from left) from the Renard edition of *Treasure Island.* Bull Montana is second from left. *Opposite bottom:* A group photograph showing Chaney (with upraised arm) and Montana (with upraised leg) from the Copp Clark edition of *Treasure Island.*

my hands, drooling over the covers and sniffing the old paper." I would emphasize, however, that there is a whole additional, and often quite surprising, layer of enjoyment to be found in actually reading the stories. Nor is this pleasure limited simply to finding "lost" scenes, or to "reconstructing" whole films that no longer exist. Many of the books are interesting reading experiences in their own right, even apart from their film connections—indeed, in many cases they are entrancing in spite of their film associations rather than because of them.

I wish to pursue this line of investigation in some detail because I've found that it has greatly increased my own appreciation of the items in the collection. The books and magazines, when viewed from unconventional angles, become much more than the mere desiccated husks of vanished or obscure motion pictures. William Hazlitt once wrote:

> The most trifling objects, retraced with the eye of memory, assume the vividness, the delicacy, and importance of insects seen through a magnifying glass.... Ask the sum-total of the value of human life, and we are puzzled with the length of the account and the multiplicity of items in it: take any one of them apart, and it is wonderful what matter of reflection will be found in it!
>
> "The Letter-Bell"

In looking at the unlikely material of this collection "through a magnifying glass," and taking it "apart," I've found that the interesting stories the books contain are by no means confined to the chapters written by their authors. I suspect that any good book collection assembled over many years, with passion, enthusiasm, serendipity, and dedication, could generate an account comparable to what follows. In any event, I hope the present volume leads other collectors to look again at their own volumes, perhaps in new ways, and thereby to enjoy them all the more.

I find the books from the 1910s, '20s, and '30s to be most interesting, as they so often reflect cultural conditions and assumptions about their world that diverge in interesting ways from contemporary sensibilities. They provide a window into a period at the very beginning of the great technological roller coaster ride that the twentieth century would become. In these volumes, people change into special "motoring togs" before getting into a car; the heroine often has a chauffeur, or gives "orders to have her runabout brought around" if she wishes to drive off by herself. This would be after her French maid brings in "the morning's mail on a salver."

In a passage in one of the mysteries, *Whispering Wires* (1918), in which the detective is trying to account for all of the people in the house, his questioning of the heroine elicits the fact that there is "a French maid," "the housekeeper," and "Father's valet." Then she adds: "There's a French chef and a pantry man, I think. Also there's a poor old darky who tends to the furnace. I don't believe he leaves the basement. I never see him, only on holidays."

The detective then goes on to mention that "The butler, then, and the doorman and the second man and the rest of the servants" have been taken already for interrogation. Nine servants singled out—"and the rest"!

A male driver in these books usually refers to his car as his "machine." In one, the narrator makes a point of noting conspicuous extravagance: "Although the sun had not yet set, the electric lights were already agleam." Electricity and electrical gadgets have a fresh wonder about them. Even doors are seen through a different lens—especially in the mystery novels, they are always assumed to have transoms. Blacks seldom figure as important characters; Germans are sometimes automatically villianized as "Huns" in the World War I era. "Orientals" are plentiful, and are usually of the lurking "Yellow Peril" stereotype. They are uniformly well-versed in navigating secret passages in dingy waterfront warehouses. The unlikely exteriors of these buildings, however, lead to unsuspected hideaways of great silken and incensed splendor, with unseen gongs conveying messages of infiltration and alarm. A century after these books were written, it is truly surprising to note how utterly taken-for-granted were the background cultural assumptions about "sinister" Orientals in the popular fiction of the time—as well as, of course, in the movies and serials to which these books are tied.

Here, for instance, are a few typical passages from these popular fiction books that convey some of their flavor, offered "warts and all" with their stereotypes of women and ethnic groups, along with the enthusiasm of their Saturday-matinee earnestness:

> His face was kindly, gentle, ineffectual; he seemed to lack the final "punch" that send men over the line to success; this was evident in the way his necktie hung, the way his thin hands fluttered. [*Seven Keys to Baldpate*, 1913]

> "... it came to me to compare that maid I knew in the long ago with the women I know to-day. Ah, gentlemen! Lips, made but for smiling, fling weighty arguments on the unoffending atmosphere. Eyes, made to light with that light that never was by land or sea, blaze instead with what they call the injustice of women's servitude. White hands, made to find their way to the hands of some young man in the moonlight, carry banners in dusty streets. It seemed

that I saw the blue eyes of that girl of long ago turned, sad, rebuking, on her sisters of to-day. As I finished reading, my heart was awhirl. I said to the young men before me:

"'There *was* a woman, gentlemen—a woman worth a million suffragettes.'

"They applauded. The fire in me died down." [*Ibid.*]

Mr. Magee pictured him on a Chautauqua platform, the white water pitcher by his side. [*Ibid.*]

"She is one of the finest weapons in the enemy's armory, Petrie! But a woman is a two-edged sword, and treacherous. To our great good fortune, she has formed a sudden predilection, characteristically Oriental, for yourself." [*The Insidious Dr. Fu Manchu*, 1913]

The dacoit swung himself below the window with the agility of an ape, as, with a dull, muffled thud, *something* dropped upon the carpet!

"Stand still, for your life!" came Smith's voice, high-pitched.

A beam of white leaped out across the room and played full upon the coffee-table in the center.

Prepared as I was for something horrible, I know that I paled at sight of the thing that was running around the edge of the envelope.

It was an insect, full six inches long, and of a vivid, venomous, red color! It had something of the appearance of a great ant, with its long, quivering antennae and its febrile, horrible vitality; but it was proportionately longer of body and smaller of head, and had numberless rapidly moving legs. In short, it was a giant centipede, apparently of the scolopendra group, but of a form quite new to me.

These things I realized in one breathless instant; in the next— Smith had dashed the thing's poisonous life out with one straight, true blow of the golf club!

* * *

"Never mind the dacoit, Petrie," he said…. "We know now what causes the mark of the Zayatt Kiss. Therefore science is richer for our first brush with the enemy, and the enemy is poorer—unless he has any more unclassified centipedes." [*Ibid.*][1]

So I shall always remember, with pleasure, that dinner-party at Redmoat, in the old-world dining room; it was so very peaceful, so almost grotesquely calm. For I, within my very bones, felt it to be the calm before the storm.

When, later, we men passed to the library, we seemed to leave that atmosphere behind us.

"Redmoat," said the Rev. J. D. Eltham, "has latterly become the theater of strange doings." [*Ibid.*]

"No," he rapped, through clenched teeth. "A servant of the Crown in the East makes his motto: 'Keep your word, though it break your neck!'" [*Ibid.*]

East and West may not intermingle. As a student of world-policies, as a physician, I admitted, could not deny, that truth. [*Ibid.*]

"Harley St. John? Well, if I catch that fop taking you motoring again you'll get your wish and see a real nice aristocratic murder." [*The Perils of Pauline*, 1914]

It was what had come to be known in his organization as the "Brotherhood of Falsers." There, in the back room of a low dive, were Dan the Dude, the emissary who had been loitering about the laboratory, a gunman, Dago Mike, a couple of women, slatterns, one known as Kitty the Hawk, and a boy of eight or ten, whom they called Billy. [*The Exploits of Elaine*, 1915]

At the same time, in a room of the adjoining house, the Clutching Hand himself was busily engaged making the most elaborate preparations for some nefarious scheme which his fertile mind had evolved. [*Ibid.*]

Long Sin, now in rich Oriental costume, was reclining on a divan smoking a strange looking pipe and playing with two pet white rats. Each white rat had a gold band around his leg, to which was connected a gold chain about a foot in length, and the chains ended in rings which were slipped over Long's little fingers. Ordinarily, he carried the pets up the capacious sleeve of each arm.

* * *

Just as a call from "509" flashed up, Long slipped the rings off his little fingers and loosened the white rats on the telephone switch-board itself.

With a shriek, the telephone system of the Coste went temporarily out of business.

The operators fled to the nearest chairs, drawing their skirts about them.

There was the greatest excitement among all the women in the corridor. Such a display of hosiery was never contemplated by even the most daring costumers. [*Ibid.*]

In the center of a devious and winding way, quite unknown to all except those who knew the innermost secrets of the Chinese quarter and even unknown to the police, there was a dingy tenement house, apparently inhabited by hardworking Chinamen, but in reality the headquarters of the notorious devil worshippers, a sect of Satanists, banned even in the Celestial Empire.

The followers of the cult comprised some of the most dangerous Chinese criminals, thugs, and assassins, besides a number of dangerous characters who belonged to various Chinese secret societies....

The room in which the uncanny rites of the devil worshippers were conducted was a large apartment decorated in Chinese style, with highly colored portraits of some of the devil deities and costly silken hangings. Beside a large dais depended a huge Chinese gong.

On the dais itself stood, or rather sat, an ugly looking figure covered with some sort of metallic plating. It almost seemed to be the mummy of a Chinaman covered with gold leaf. It was thin and shrunken, entirely nude. [*Ibid.*]

Wu had immediately established himself in the most sumptuous of apartments, hidden behind the squalid exterior of the ordinary tenement building in Chinatown. [*The Romance of Elaine*, 1916]

Smith continued: "You *know* that she is utterly false, yet a glance or two from those dark eyes of hers can make a fool of you! A woman made a fool of me, once; but I learned my lesson; you have failed to learn yours. If you are determined to go to pieces on the rock that broke up Adam, do so! But don't involve me in the wreck, Petrie—for that might mean a yellow emperor of the world, and you know it!" [*The Return of Dr. Fu Manchu*, 1916]

Abel Slattin shrugged his shoulders, racially, and returned to the armchair which he had just quitted.... I covertly studied our visitor. He lay back in the armchair, his heavy eyelids lowered deceptively. He was a thought overdressed—a big man, dark-haired and well-groomed, who toyed with a monocle most unsuitable to his type.... with unerring Semitic instinct he had sought an opening in this glittering Rialto. [*Ibid.*]

"That was when I found out you were partly German. I got over it, though." [*Whispering Wires*, 1918]

He feared a woman and a gun more than anything else in the world. Both were liable to form a dangerous combination. [*Ibid.*]

"... we're on the trail by everyday, up-to-date methods which never fail if they are continued long enough and men work hard enough." [*Ibid.*]

"I'll shoot that cur! He's a whispering snake! A Hun!" [*Ibid.*]

"They have threatened me like they threatened poor father. They sent a letter. Oh, I wish I were a man!" [*Ibid.*]

They went to the back of the shop. The Chinese clapped his hands, and a panel in the wall slid back, disclosing a stairway. The newcomer stepped through the aperture and the panel closed behind him. He mounted the stairs and came to a room, magnificent in its Oriental splendor.

Priceless rugs covered the floor and walls, while on wonderfully carved teakwood stands reposed ancient porcelains, specimens of bygone dynasties, antique arms and armor cunningly wrought, jades and ivories marvelously fashioned by master craftsmen long since dead. Seen through the filmy haze of rising incense, the room was a veritable treasure-house of Oriental art. [*The Master Mystery*, 1919][2]

Eva practiced all those little kindnesses which are known only to women, and tears were in her eyes as she stroked his poor gray head.

How terrible was it that, after all they had attempted, all that they had suffered, they should still stand defeated in their aim to get the antidote that would cure her father's malady. However, the brave girl was not one to admit herself beaten, and even as she sat there she was planning new ways to discover who were her terrible adversaries and to bring defeat to them. [*Ibid.*]

A light of triumph came into Paul's eyes. Eva's happiness, even her life, meant nothing to him. She was merely a means to his own evil ends and he now felt sure that he held her in his grasp. Besides, in so far as such a selfish nature can care for another human being, Paul cared for De Luxe Dora. There was a fascination for him in her tigerish, unscrupulous nature that a good woman could never inspire. [*Ibid.*]

Without warning Ken sailed in. It was some scrap, for Hank had the advantage in age. But Ken had lived sensibly and clean and his motto for trouble was "Be prepared." He was a splendid boxer. Easton had taught him some football and wrestling, too.

Ken had expected it and was not disappointed—Hank was not one to fight fair. When one encounters his like one must be prepared for all sorts of mucker tricks. Ken was, and Hank got away with none of it. Instead, in about as sharp an encounter as Hank had ever experienced in his short life the bully was worsted. [*The Radio Detective*, 1926]

Indeed, the Scout world, especially along the shores of Long Island Sound, both in Long Island and in Connecticut, was being mobilized for action. And everybody who knows anything at all knows that when you want action, when you want to know anything, the place to go is the Boy Scouts. [*Ibid.*]

Far off on another part of the Sound was a couple in a small cruiser with the name *Sea Vamp*. They had the radio fever. Off and on as they idled from harbor to harbor they would amuse themselves by turning on the radio.... Here was a thrill that for a moment caught their jazz-jaded attention. The woman, especially, was excited. [*Ibid.*]

> The fact of the matter was, however, that Rae and Jack Curtis were as safe with the mysterious skipper of the *Scooter* as a paraffin cat chased by an asbestos dog in Hades.... It was a bitter pill for those smart young criminals to swallow, to realize that they were merely little cogs in a machine, that the gears had been stripped and they were slated for the scrap heap. [*Ibid.*]

> "Well, man or woman, old or young, ugly or beautiful, we're after you, and we are going to get you. We have our reputations to live up to, you know; and the C.I.D. of Scotland Yard must always get its man—or woman." [*London After Midnight*, 1928]

> "Pull yourself together, now," he urged earnestly. "Listen here, little girl. I'll take care of that boy no matter what the cost. You can count on me! I'll stand by you! I'll see him through!" [*The Spider*, 1929]

> They looked under-nourished, unbathed, and slovenly clad. Their very carriage, their shifty eyes, the nervous scarred fingers, fiddling with their battered felt hats; every detail of their appearance advertised them as men one could never trust—as the sort of men one would hate to meet in a dark alley late at night. Yet, withal, they were pathetic. Certainly, they had been but tools in whatever conspiracy—the men could hardly have passed an intelligence test of immigrants! [*Ibid.*]

I do not mean to imply that all of the books in the collection are written at this level; authors such as Arthur Conan Doyle, H. G. Wells, Robert Louis Stevenson, Edgar Allan Poe, and Nathaniel Hawthorne are included, too. Nevertheless, from the cultural perspective of the early 2000s, one's jaw simply drops during the reading of many of these volumes. When one is exposed to the extent and prevalence of the common attitudes of the time, prejudices taken utterly for granted by a majority of all parties, then the social and political advances of the last century can be appreciated all the more, in contrast. These books really are a kind of time machine. Much academic writing at present is concerned, of course, with delineating the oppressiveness of these older popular assumptions in the now fashionable realms of study demarcated by race, class, and gender; the delineation is usually accompanied with an implied judgment that the oppressors of a century ago should simply have known better. I suspect, however, that readers exposed to these old novels directly, rather than to the academic treatises about them, might gain insight into the reality of the encumbrances as well as a greater understanding of both the pervasiveness of their presence and the absence of perceived alternatives in so much of popular culture.

In any event, the fact that these old novels show us even "right thinking" heroes and heroines indulging in thinking that, by today's standards, can be regarded only as stereotypical is not terribly surprising. What may be more interesting is the consideration of how readers a century from our own time may regard our own popular fiction: what blind spots in our understanding of human rights and social justice will seem similarly naive a century from now? What, for example, will be the next century's verdict on our current "political correctness"? Will our present views on affirmative action, homosexuality, or abortion seem quaint in 2104? Will readers of the future regard prejudices against Muslims in the same way we now look back at World War I era views of Germans? Will our current fears of the "clash of civilizations" be as denigrated then as "Yellow Peril" hysteria is now? Will deconstruction and postmodernism be seen as passing intellectual fads comparable to anarchism, Freudianism, or Marxism? Will our own infatuation with the Internet be regarded then in the same way we look back at "radio fever" now? And what new technology will fill that same addictive niche in the future? I've made a speculative list for myself, but will refrain from offering it here since my own crystal ball has no special claim to merit in this area. What I would suggest to other collectors, though, is to consider their own books in a similar light—there is much more of interest in these old volumes than just their photo illustrations.

The evidence for these older worldviews shows up not just in the stories contained in the books, but in the publishers' notices, advertisements, and promotional lists that often follow the texts of the novels.

For example, the overall aim of the popular fiction so well represented in these photoplay books is rather well delineated in a particular full page ad that appears in several of them:

> The greatest pleasure in life is that of reading. Why not then own the books of great novelists when the price is so small

---

> Of all the amusements which can possibly be imagined for a hard-working man, after his daily toil, or in its intervals, there is nothing like reading an entertaining book. It calls for no bodily exertion. It transports him into a livelier, and gayer, and more diversified and interesting scene, and while he enjoys himself there he may forget the evils of the present moment. Nay, it accompanies him to his next day's work, and gives him something to think of besides the mere mechanical drudgery of his every-day occupation—something he can enjoy while absent, and look forward with pleasure to return to.

Ask your dealer for a list of the titles in Burt's Popular Priced Fiction

---

In buying the books bearing the A. L. Burt Company imprint
you are assured of wholesome, entertaining and instructive reading

The implied audience here is one of men working in blue-collar occupations requiring physical labor, and whose intellects are largely stifled by the monotony of their jobs. (The world of these readers was certainly not that of the "service economy" of a century later, in which a college education is taken for granted.) Indeed, the wording of the ad very much mirrors the then-contemporary social concern of the "alienation of labor" so central to the popular flirtation with, if not outright embrace of, socialism and fellow-traveling in the 1920s and '30s. Not that these novels, or their ads, are Marxist screeds—they are not; but they do offer insights into the popular perception of working class life of the time, and some of its real discontents. This particular ad is an interesting sketch of the assumed conditions of the population being targeted by these books; it happened also that these same conditions made socialism seem, at the time, to be a viable remedy to the alienation caused by the "mechanical drudgery" of assembly-line capitalism. The assumption that the latter was a common condition of the audience's lives suggests, too, a baseline awareness of distinctions among social classes that is greater than we have today; the pervasiveness of this assumption is evidenced repeatedly in the novels themselves.

The overall point is that the justification for "reading an entertaining book" is here presented in terms of relief or therapeutic distraction for downtrodden workers, as the road to an alternative imaginative world in which they can escape, rather than as a means to form and broaden their awareness and understanding, the better to perceive and to deal with the problems of the world in which they actually live. That such an escapist world does not require difficult or unaccustomed moral or political judgments, other than merely to distinguish "good guys" from "bad guys," is a given. These books generally present worlds in which one can simply relax and "go with the flow," just as it is presented, without any need to critically question then-current notions of justice, equality, or relations between the sexes.

Many of the books present several pages of advertisements for other novels, in lists appended after the host-volume's story is finished. Although some of the lists advertise writers whose works are still read today (Edgar Rice Burroughs, Jack London, and Zane Grey among them), most offer popular-fiction authors of the time who are probably read nowadays, if at all, only by those who share either the zealotry of a collector, or the despair of a graduate student who realizes that these are the only writers left who haven't already been picked over. Some of these ads read as follows; the first two are appended to *He Who Gets Slapped* (1925), the next follows *London After Midnight* (1928), and the last appears in *Charlie Chan Carries On* (1930):

RUBY M. AYRES' NOVELS

May be had wherever books are sold. Ask for Grosset & Dunlap's list.

THE MAN WITHOUT A HEART
Why was Barbara held captive in a deserted hermit's hut for days by a "man without a heart" and in the end how was it that she held the winning cards.

THE MATHERSON MARRIAGE
She married for money. With her own hands she had locked the door on happiness and thrown away the key. But, read the story which is very interesting and well told.
[I *love* that "well, regardless" comma after "But"!—T.M.]

RICHARD CHATTERTON
A fascinating story in which love and jealousy play strange tricks with women's souls.

A BACHELOR HUSBAND
Can a woman love two men at the same time?
In its solving of this particular variety of triangle "A Bachelor Husband" will particularly interest, and strangely enough, without one shock to the most conventional minded.

THE SCAR
With fine comprehension and insight the author shows a terrific contrast between the woman whose love was of the flesh and one whose love was of the spirit.

WINDS OF THE WORLD
Jill, a poor little typist, marries the great Henry Sturgess and inherits millions, but not happiness. Then at last—but we must leave that to Ruby M. Ayres to tell you as only she can.

THE SECOND HONEYMOON
In this story the author has produced a book which no one who has loved or hopes to love can afford to miss. The story fairly leaps from climax to climax.

STORIES OF RARE CHARM BY
GENE STRATTON-PORTER

May be had wherever books are sold. Ask for Grosset & Dunlap's list.

HER FATHER'S DAUGHTER.
This story is of California and tells of that charming girl, Linda Strong, otherwise known as "Her Father's Daughter."

A DAUGHTER OF THE LAND.
Kate Bates, the heroine of this story, is a true "Daughter of the Land," and to read about her is truly inspiring.

MICHAEL O'HALLORAN.
Michael is a quick-witted little Irish newsboy, living in Northern Indiana. He adopts a deserted little girl, a cripple. He also aspires to lead the entire rural community upward and onward.

LADDIE.
This is a bright, cheery tale with scenes laid in Indiana. The story is told by Little Sister, the youngest member of a large family, but it is concerned not so much with childish doings as with the love affairs of older members of the family.

A GIRL OF THE LIMBERLOST.
The story of a girl of the Michigan woods; a buoyant, loveable type of the self-reliant American. Her philosophy is one of love and kindness toward all things; her hope is never dimmed.

AT THE FOOT OF THE RAINBOW.
The scene of this charming love story is laid in Central Indiana. It is one of devoted friendship, and tender and self-sacrificing love.

THE NOVELS OF TEMPLE BAILEY

May be had wherever books are sold. Ask for Grosset & Dunlap's list.

THE BLUE WINDOW
The heroine, Hildegarde, finds herself transplanted from the middle western farm to the gay social whirl of the East. She is almost swept off her feet, but in the end proves true blue.

PEACOCK FEATHERS
The eternal conflict between wealth and love. Jerry, the idealist who is poor, loves Mimi, a beautiful, spoiled society girl.

THE TRUMPETER SWAN
Randy Paine comes back from France to the monotony of every-day affairs. But the girl he loves shows him the beauty in the common place.

THE TIN SOLDIER
   A man who wishes to serve his country, but is bound by a tie he cannot in honor break—that's Derry. A girl who loves him, shares his humiliation and helps him to win—that's Jean. Their love is the story.

NOVELS OF MAY CHRISTIE
THRILLING STORIES OF THE MODERN GIRL

May be had wherever books are sold. Ask for Grosset & Dunlap's list.

THE JAZZ WIDOW
   The story of a handsome widow who inherited a fortune and set out to find youth and love in Paris. It remained for her daughter to show what true love is.

LOVE'S MIRACLE
   Business to Jane meant tea dancing and dinner at the Ritz—night clubs and champagne. She was a success—but the man she loved said she was trading in love.

A KISS FOR CORINNA
   Corinna is in love with a man who is pursued by a pleasure seeking society girl—and the irony of the situation is that it is her duty to make this girl beautiful. A fascinating story of the twists and turns in rivalry and love.

LOVE'S ECSTASY
   A little stenographer fighting for her love against a fascinating young mistress of millions. A duel of feminine wits and wiles that you will follow with burning interest. It is a romance of surprising twists and turns.

The ads for "women's books" share space equally with those for men; and among the frequent notices for books by Edgar Rice Burroughs and Zane Grey one occasionally finds a particularly topical list, as appended to *Behind That Curtain* (1928):

STIRRING TALES OF THE GREAT WAR

May be had wherever books are sold. Ask for Grosset & Dunlap's list.

WAR BIRDS   The Diary of an Unknown Aviator
   Soaring, looping, zooming, spitting hails of leaden death, planes everywhere in a war darkened sky. WAR BIRDS is a tale of youth, loving, fighting, dying.

WINGS   John Monk Saunders
   Based on the great Paramount picture, WINGS is the Big Parade

of the air, the gallant, fascinating story of an American air
pilot.

LEAVE ME WITH A SMILE   Elliott W. Springs
   Henry Winton, a famous ace, thrice decorated, twice wounded
and many times disillusioned returns after the war to meet Phyllis,
one of the new order of hard-drinking, unmoral girls.

NOCTURNE MILITAIRE   Elliott White Springs
   War, with wine and women, tales of love, madness, heroism;
flyers reckless in their gestures toward life and death.

CHEVRONS   Leonard Nason
   One of the sensations of the post-war period, CHEVRONS dis-
closes the whole pageantry of war with grim truth flavored with the
breezy vulgarity of soldier dialogue.

In a sense, one appreciates the achievements of Hemingway and Fitzger-
ald all the more when one realizes how large was the field of other literature on the "disillusioned" and "hard-drinking" men and women of
the postwar period. The recurrence of several themes just in these brief
advertisements—inherited wealth, lowly typists, spoiled society girls,
"true blue" morality persisting in the face of a new order—all open a
window on the general culture of the period, and its new and very real
tensions between the "conventional minded" and the "reckless."
     Apart from what might be called the social views of these old
books, there are equally apparent changes in matters of aesthetic taste.
Two examples in particular leap out from this collection. One concerns
the Philo Vance mysteries written by S. S. Van Dine (a pseudonym of
Willard Huntington Wright, 1888-1939); the other, the popularity of
"old house thrillers" as a mystery-horror genre.
     The Philo Vance stories could not be written today any more than
the Fu Manchu novels of Sax Rohmer, although for different reasons.
(The Rohmer name is another pseudonym, for Arthur Henry Sarsfield
Ward, 1883-1959.) The latter thrillers are classics of the Yellow Peril
stereotype; their portrayals of women are much in the same vein, as the
excerpts above demonstrate. Whereas Sax Rohmer's social views strike
contemporary readers—at least those unwilling to suspend the disbelief needed to read the stories—as grating, Van Dine's Philo Vance character comes across today as just amusingly outlandish. Vance is a rich
gentleman-playboy—although largely sexless—in the gilded New York
of the 1920s and '30s; he smokes gold-tipped *Régie* cigarettes from a
Florentine humidor, drives a Hispano-Suiza, indulges in "matutinal
Turkish coffee," and evinces polymath expertise in art, antiquities, chess,

languages, mythology, ethnology, dog breeds, gambling probabilities, astronomy, seventeenth century philosophy, the higher mathematics, and other arcana. Indeed, just as one looks forward, in the Sherlock Holmes stories, to the distinctive instances of Holmes's clever inferences from a hat, a watch, or a walking-stick, in the Vance stories one similarly comes to expect the detective's gratuitous digressions, in great scholarly detail, on Chinese porcelains or tropical fish cultivation. He investigates crime as a hobby, in the company of his friends District Attorney Markham and the Watson-like amanuensis Van Dine.

The prose of the novels tends very much toward the purple end of the spectrum, being heavily larded with terms such as "diabolical," "cunning," "fiendish," "grotesque," "devilish," and "orgy of horror." The aristocratic Vance routinely truncates words ("Don't y' know," "Amazin'") and exclaims things like "Tosh!," "'Pon my soul," "Tut, tut, my good man!," "Deuced clever!," and "Perpend, Markham." In the course of pursuing the killer in *The Greene Murder Case*, he throws out lines such as: "Alas, Sergeant, I've been immersed in the terra-cotta ornamentation of Renaissance facades, and other such trivialities, since I saw you last"; and "Ah, well, there's nothing for me to do while you Jasons are launched on your quaint quest. I think I'll retire and resume my translation of Delacroix's 'Journal.'"

Vance also habitually manifests an expertise in the "cranial formations" of individuals—in one of the mysteries, he eliminates a suspect from consideration because of the shape of his head. While phrenology has not survived the 1920s as a science, its presence in these old books lends it the charm of a strange, ancient insect embedded in amber.

The stories are routinely set in upper-crust Manhattan mansions; usually, they provide detailed foldout diagrams showing cut-away architectural plans of the various apartments, passages, stairs, chiffoniers, and portières (rather than mere doors). The sinister atmospherics of the houses, beneath their sumptuous accoutrements, are customarily dwelt on at length, as in *The Dragon Murder Case* and *The Greene Murder Case*:

> "The answer to the whole problem lies somewhere in the Stamm residence. That's a strange place, Markham. It's full of infinite possibilities—with its distorted traditions, its old superstitions, and its stagnant air of a dead and buried age, its insanity and decadence, and its folklore and demonology. Such a place produces strange quirks of mind: even casual visitors are caught in its corroding

atmosphere. Such an atmosphere generates and begets black and incredible crimes. You have seen, in the last two days, how every one with whom we have talked was poisoned by these subtle and sinister influences."

"That house is polluted, Markham. It's crumbling in decay—not material decay, perhaps, but a putrefaction far more terrible. The very heart and essence of that old house is rotting away. And all the inmates are rotting with it, disintegrating in spirit and mind and character. They've been polluted by the very atmosphere they've created. This crime, which you take so lightly, was inevitable in such a setting. I only wonder it was not more terrible, more vile. It marked one of the tertiary stages of the general dissolution of that abnormal establishment."

The suspects—and victims—in the books are usually as sumptuously appointed as the mansions they inhabit. The stories are replete to surfeit with the details of a gilded world to which they invited their Depression-era readers; another passage from the *Dragon* story is typical:

The inspection of Greeff's belongings took but a short time. Vance went first to the clothes-closet and found there a brown business suit and a sport suit; but the pockets held nothing of any importance. The dinner suit was then investigated, without any enlightening result: its pockets contained merely an ebony cigarette holder, a cigarette case of black moiré silk, and two elaborately monogrammed handkerchiefs. There was nothing belonging to Greeff in the drawers of the dressing-table; and in the cabinet of the bathroom were only the usual toilet accessories—a toothbrush and paste, a shaving outfit, a bottle of toilet water and a shaker of talcum powder. Nor did the Gladstone bag yield anything significant or suggestive.

An earlier inspection of another male victim's bedroom had noted, "Over the foot of the colonial bed hung a suit of mauve silk pajamas, and on a chair nearby had been thrown a purple surah silk dressing-gown"; after which Vance remarked, "Everything's quite conventional and in order.... I fear we'll have to look elsewhere for clues." This is a fantasy world for working-class readers, in which silk, monograms, and separate suits for dinner are taken for granted, and ebony is a "mere" throwaway detail.

The tone of the books is further exemplified by Vance's interchanges with his customary ally, Markham, as in snippets from *The "Canary" Murder Case* and *The Dragon Murder Case*:

"What new harlequinade is this?"
"Fie on you! Answer my question."

"Every factor in it that we try to touch turns into a sort of *Fata Morgana*...."
"Don't give way to discouragement, old dear," Vance consoled him. "It's not as Cimmerian as it appears."

Unlike the situation with the Fu Manchu books, the unconventional elements in the Vance novels strike one now as more quaintly eccentric than jarring, as they are more aesthetic and stylistic than socially or ethically substantive. Not that any of these mysteries are substantive to begin with; it's just that a portrait centered on the extremities of Vance's upper class aestheticism is less discordant nowadays than one comparably centered on racial prejudice. In the final analysis, the books continue to be enjoyable, all the more so for being period pieces whose affections could not be appealed to by authors writing today.

Still, the books are enjoyable, all the more for being period pieces whose affectations could not be appealed to by authors writing today.

Other mysteries prominent in the collection also come across now as period pieces of a different sort; they are often referred to as "old house thrillers" or "old dark house" mysteries. Included in this group are such stories as *The Bat* and *The Gorilla*, which usually feature secret panels, clutching hands, and horribly-masked or disfigured villains. The genre, with many variations, usually revolves around a few basic plots:

A. Greedy heirs, often in formal evening dress, assembling for the reading of a will in a spooky old house, as in *The Cat and the Canary*.

B. Innocent new owners or renters of a spooky old house being terrorized by a master criminal, or gang of criminals, trying to scare them away from a treasure hidden within it, as in *The Bat* or *Hold That Ghost*.

C. Innocent travelers being forced by a terrible storm to seek shelter in a spooky old house, occupied by a madman or a monster, when the bridge or the road ahead has been washed away, as in *The Old Dark House* or *The Black Cat*.

D. Guilty associates in, or perpetrators of, past crimes being summoned to an old house, where revenge or justice is wrought upon them sequentially, as in *And Then There Were None* or *The Rogues' Tavern*.

E. A young woman, on the verge of her legal coming-of-age birthday, being summoned to an old mansion to become, at midnight, the official heir to the family fortune, and being threatened by a guardian or alternate heir, as in *Topper Returns* or *You'll Find Out*.

What distinguishes the films in this genre (to which the photoplay stories are tied) even more than their plots, however, are what may be called their atmospheric accoutrements: the many scenic elements and bits of business that tend to show up in clusters, the simple recognition of which provides a kind of aesthetic satisfaction in itself, that of seeing an expected form filling itself out with unexpected variations of tried-and-true material. Taken together, these form a kind of predictable "Periodic Table of Elements":

- secret panels (especially in bookcases) with horrible clutching hands reaching out from them; grandfather clocks and tombs often provide other openings to hidden passages
- secret rooms
- control rooms with equipment for either monitoring or scaring house occupants
- trapdoors
- turntable wall panels
- chairs that hold occupants with iron bands, or dump them into secret rooms or wells
- old paintings with removable eye-holes for spying
- horribly masked killers in slouch hats or hooded robes
- disguised master criminals named after some scary animal
- criminals who leave "signature" notes at their crime scenes
- a hero who is comically cowardly, but who proves to be courageous in the outcome
- the dead man's will being conveyed to the greedy heirs by a voice recording of the dead man himself
- sinister housekeepers
- manservants or butlers wearing turbans
- mobile suits of armor
- gorillas on the loose
- maps with missing pieces
- warning notes wrapped around rocks and thrown through windows
- the playing of an old organ causing a door to open to a secret passage
- chandeliers or flower pots that fall and just miss the heroine
- fabulous missing gems
- mysterious rappings on walls
- séances at which someone gets murdered
- telephone lines mysteriously cut

- guests in the old house switching rooms, resulting in the wrong person being attacked during the night
- maniacs escaped from asylums or prisons
- detectives who always wear their hats indoors
- faked confinements to wheelchairs
- faked deaths and burials
- faked limps or bent postures that are maintained by the villain even when no one is watching
- disappearing and reappearing corpses, and
- thunderstorms.

Often the words *Night* or *Midnight* appear in the titles of these movies. Satanic cults tend to show up in type C films; quaintly dated nightclub acts sometimes enliven type B stories, especially if the comedy element is strong. Comedy at the low end of the scale includes standard bits such as a moving candle on the back of a tortoise; or a jumping hat or skull propelled by a frog or an owl inside; or someone's coat becoming hooked to a mounted skeleton (or suit of armor), which then follows the person. Sometimes the ending of the movie features a direct address from the villain to the audience not to reveal who he is. Ethnic stereotypes are also customary: a black butler, "Man Friday" valet, or chauffeur who is scared of ghosts (often engagingly played by Willie Best with more humor and sly intelligence than the parts merit); or a generic "sinister Oriental" predictably peering in, slyly, through a window or listening at a door. Sometimes there is a grumpy "battle axe" elderly woman; occasionally, too, a maid who is afraid of ghosts. The fast-talking hero is frequently a reporter; in my own checklist, the film gets double points if he is played by Wallace Ford. "Brassy" women reporters sometimes appear as leads, too. If he's not a reporter, the hero is often a "radio detective" who solves on his radio program crimes that have baffled police. Sometimes the heroes are played by comedy teams. The stock sinister butler is usually played by Bela Lugosi. (Double points, again, if Lugosi is also wearing a turban; an additional point if Lionel Atwill is anywhere in the cast, and a half-point for the presence of the poverty-row star Mischa Auer.)

Films in this genre present endless possibilities for combining the same spooky elements; watching a lot of them involves a certain lowbrow connoisseurship (an oxymoronic distinction in itself), somewhat like being able to appreciate the variations of chess games, except that the patterns here are narrative rather than spatial. (As Miss Jean Brodie put it so well, in a different context, "For those who like that sort of thing ... that is the sort of thing they like.")

Any number of these films or plays have generated book tie-ins, such as *And Then There Were None, The Bat, The Bat Whispers, The Cat and the Canary, The Ghost Breaker, The Greene Murder Case, The Master Mind, The Master Mystery, The Old Dark House, Seven Keys to Baldpate, Silent House, Temple Tower, The Terror, The 13th Hour,* and *Whispering Wires.* Magazine stories of such films are also numerous, including "The Black Cat" (both 1934 and 1941 versions), "The Cat Creeps" (1930) in two fictionized versions, "A Face in the Fog," "The Ghost and Mr. Chicken," "The Ghost Breakers," "The Ghost Catchers," "The Gorilla" (1927 and 1939), "Hold That Ghost!" (1941) in two versions, "The House of Mystery," "The Laurel-Hardy Murder Mystery," "Return of The Terror," "The Rogues' Tavern," "Secret of the Blue Room," "A Shot in the Dark," "The Thirteenth Chair," "The 13th Guest," "The 13th Hour," "Topper Returns," "The Unholy Night," "Whispering Ghosts," and "You'll Find Out."

"The Unholy Night" story in *Screen Book Magazine* of January 1930 is a typical example. Many of these old house thrillers used the word "Night" in their titles—*Night of Terror, One Exciting Night, One Frightened Night*—and so, right there, this story fills a proper niche in the "Periodic Table" of predictable plot elements; but it also includes heirs to a will, a murderous and scarred madman, a séance with a murder, and a sinister Asian servant. What is most interesting is that the servant in the film version is played not by Bela Lugosi (who often played the role in the 1930s), but by Boris Karloff (who played similar turban-wearing servants in 1920s films such as *The Hope Diamond Mystery* and *Behind That Curtain*, an early Charlie Chan film).

Karloff also appears in the illustrations to "Behind The Mask" in the June 18, 1932, issue of the British film magazine *Boy's Cinema*. This story features photos of him together with Edward Van Sloan, who, in this plot, plays a villainous, disguised mad doctor. This role was quite unlike his more famous appearances as the wise and elderly opponent to Karloff's monsters in both *Frankenstein* and *The Mummy*. Although filmed before *Frankenstein, Behind the Mask* was not released until afterwards. It is just the kind of title a collector in this field most relishes, bringing to light as it does a whole, and otherwise quite obscure, "stratum" in a screen relationship of classic genre actors.

As noted earlier, many of the films represented by these books or magazine stories are now completely lost. One of the most famous of all lost films, in fact, is *The Terror*, which was not only an "old dark house" thriller, but was also the very first talkie horror film, in 1928. A photoplay novelization survives, however; the dust jacket of this British tie-in book shows a black-robed and hooded figure carrying a girl down a stairway; the back cover shows the same spooky figure with raised arms terrorizing the girl in front of large pipe organ. The inside flap of its jacket says:

> A sensational success as a play, [*The Terror*] has been made into an exciting film, and now comes the book to provide hours of wonderful reading for all who enjoy a first-rate detective story in Edgar Wallace's characteristic style. Follow the unraveling of the mystery of the lonely house throughout whose dark corridors echoed the strange notes of a church organ. Where did it come from and who played it? Who was the hooded form which swept down in the night unseen upon its prey and dragged its victims to destruction?

One of the excellent reference books in the genre, Roy Kinnard's *Horror in Silent Films* (McFarland, 1995), says of this story, "Adapted from a derivative mystery play by Edgar Wallace, *The Terror* dealt with a *Phantom of the Opera*–type maniac who terrorizes guests in an isolated English mansion." The novel is indeed a story of stolen treasure hidden in an old manor house with secret rooms and passages, and of a black-robed master criminal maniac who terrorizes the boarders in the house. The movie edition, while not having any actual photographs from the film, does have ten wonderfully atmospheric woodcut illustrations, seven of which have captions that are taken directly from particular passages in the novel; indeed, these captions include notes in tiny print explicitly saying "*See page 83* [and *96, 170, 171, 171* (again), *178,* and *190*]" for the corresponding section of the text. Three of these elaborate illustrations, however, have neither correspondences to the text of the novel nor notes to "*See*" any particular page; they are therefore very probably depictions of scenes from the lost film adaptation.

The illustration on page 113, especially—a picture of a man holding what is apparently a lifelike copy of another man's head —is of an incident that bears no resemblance to anything at all in the text of the novel; it therefore must be providing us with a tantalizing glimpse of a scene from the lost motion picture.

A follow-up movie, *Return of The Terror*, appeared in 1934; it featured Mary Astor, Lyle Talbot, Frank McHugh as the brash reporter, and a host of regulars from other horror or "old house" films appearing in supporting roles: J. Carroll Naish, Frank Reicher, Irving Pichel, and

Dust jacket from *The Terror*

Charles Grapewin. Film reference books maintain this version is actually a remake rather than a sequel; but having read the fictionized versions of both, I can say the stories are barely related to each other. Each has a "madman" terrorizing people; but that is the extent of similarity.

A sidelight on *The Terror* is worth mentioning, simply because I suspect it will resonate with other collectors. This novel is the only Edgar Wallace mystery I have ever read. Although Wallace was a prolific mystery writer in the 1920s, and many of his stories were made into films, *The Terror* is the only Edgar Wallace–authored movie edition I have ever found. Nevertheless, over the years I have eagerly grabbed for many a "non-photoplay" Wallace mystery on bookstore shelves—because their bindings are very similar in appearance to the Grosset & Dunlap and A. L. Burt books that actually are photoplays. After some years as a collector, in which I developed the knack of being able to spot, quickly, likely photoplay volumes among many others, just from their bindings, I eventually developed the even more refined skill of *not* reaching for the Edgar Wallace books. (Among collectors this is somewhat comparable to developing the attenuated aesthetic sensibility of a Roderick Usher.) What I had never realized, however, is that—to my great surprise—Wallace was actually a pretty good writer (at least by the standards of the genre). He plays well with the "old house" conventions. *The Terror*, after four decades of collecting, finally gave me a reason to like Edgar Wallace, instead of being habitually disappointed when my eye was drawn to one of his volumes on a bookstore shelf.

There is no simple answer to the question of why old house thrillers

See page 178.

She was paralysed with fear and could not move.

F

The Terror

She shrank back against the bed-post.

The Terror

" Do you recognise him ? "

The Terror

flourished in the decades before World War II and then quickly disappeared thereafter. It is perhaps noteworthy that their basic plots entail the assumption that "evil" in whatever guise—murder, greed, madness, revenge—is something not experienced in the normal course of the characters' lives; rather, it is something that is localized in out-of-the-

The Monk's Door.

The Terror

ordinary places (spooky old houses), and in out-of-the-ordinary circumstances (involving will readings of eccentric millionaires, washed out
roads, hidden loot). It is also interesting that lust or sexual desire is, in
general, conspicuously absent as a motivating force in suspects' doings.
In other words, evil is not something that is an everyday part of life; it
is more like an exotic element of a artificial game played within the
definite limits of a circumscribed gameboard, marked by other equally
exotic elements (secret passages, masked figures, suits of armor) that are
also not found outside the artificial space. The evil of these stories is
more aesthetic than moral, more artificial than real, more of an enter-
tainment than an insight into real life. William K. Everson makes a
telling comment on film mysteries in his book *The Detective in Film*
(Citadel Press, 1972), that

> up to the mid-forties, the words "murder" and "mystery" recur most
> frequently in titles. After about 1947 there is a shift and, strangely
> enough, among the oft-used words now are "street" and "city" (as in
> *The Sleeping City, The Street with No Name, The Naked City*). Crime
> has somehow become urbanized: the emphasis is not on the indi-
> vidual murderer, but on the layers of political graft and organized
> crime uncovered by the investigation of a single crime [p. 86].

One could say that in the post–World War II sensibility the bound-
aries of the gameboard were shattered: evil was no longer localized to
extraordinary settings or limited to unusual circumstances; it was all-
pervasive and apt to enmesh anyone in any locale, especially in one's
everyday life. It became realistic, urban, commonplace, gritty, and played
out in daylight, rather than being confined to midnight settings in
remote mansions, associated with exotic attributes, and clearly demarcated from the normal. Moreover, the sources of the evil became more
diffuse—from horribly scarred (and easily discernible) individuals wearing black capes and slouch hats to everyday neighbors and associates in
business suits and street clothes. The old house thrillers with their game-
boards of highly stylized conventions are indeed period pieces of a more
innocent time; but that fact lends them an even greater charm today—
especially in contrast to the later film noir genre with its sexually charged
femmes fatales, and in even greater contrast to the subsequent, and even
more radical, shift of cultural sensibilities towards the "slasher," "splatter," and gore-filled films of the post-1970 era. The latter shift indicated an ethical assumption that evil is not merely pervasive or
commonplace in daily life, but dominant and irredeemable in a nihilistic universe; it also indicated an aesthetic orientation aimed toward

shocks of disgust rather than *frissons* of fear. (In this regard, one notes that recent, and excellent, horror films of director M. Night Shyamalan, such as *The Sixth Sense* and *Signs*, mark a noticeable return to the older tradition of stories that end in a satisfying restoration of moral order— worked out, too, in a relatively believable world, not within mere game-boards of artificial conventions; and, further, accomplished with skillful directorial manipulation of atmospheric elements rather than by crude presentations of explicit gore. One can only hope, devoutly, that the box office success of these films will serve to redirect the pendulum of the genre back from its *Night of the Living Dead* and "splatter" extremes.)

Beyond the traditional photoplay books and magazine story tie-ins, an equally interesting area lies in genre novels that are tied to plays (rather than films), illustrated with photos from the stage productions. Play scripts themselves, too, were often published with photo-illustrations. A particularly valuable instance is *The Merry Men and Other Tales and Fables* by Robert Louis Stevenson, published by Charles Scribner's Sons in 1917. This volume includes *Strange Case of Dr. Jekyll and Mr. Hyde* and is illustrated with a lone double-exposure photo of Richard Mansfield as both Jekyll and Hyde. Mansfield was the first actor ever to play the role; he originated it onstage in 1887. Indeed, his play was on the boards in London in 1888 at exactly the same time the Jack the Ripper murders were taking place.[3]

An example of a particularly scarce illustrated play-script is the 1927 Samuel French publication of *Dracula*, with photographs from the original Broadway stage production with Bela Lugosi in the lead and Edward Van Sloan as his elderly nemesis Van Helsing, four years before they made the classic film together.

The Bat and *The Cat and the Canary*, the two main progenitors of the "old house thriller" genre, also exist not just as tie-in novels but as photo-illustrated play-scripts. The latter title includes photos of its author John Willard and actor Henry Hull in the cast. (Hull has other horror-mystery associations: In the same year as *The Cat* onstage, he appeared in D.W. Griffith's film *One Exciting Night*, which is yet another old house thriller; he also went on to play the lead in the *Werewolf of London* movie a decade later—for which there is a tie-in magazine story.) Three different, and very scarce, editions of *The Ghost Breaker* also exist, with photos from its original 1913 stage production; one is a script, two are novelizations of the story. H. B. Warner, who starred in the play, also starred in a lost 1914 film version. A permutation of this script eventually served as the basis of the classic 1940 horror-comedy with

Bela Lugosi with Edward Van Sloan (far left) in the Broadway stage production of *Dracula.*

Bob Hope and Paulette Goddard; it was then remade yet again in 1953 as a Dean Martin and Jerry Lewis comedy, *Scared Stiff.*

Arsenic and Old Lace, with photos of Boris Karloff in the comic role of the villain Jonathan Brewster, also exists in a play tie-in edition. This script contains Brewster's famous line, offered as an explanation of why he killed one of his victims, "He said I looked like Boris Karloff." (Emil Petaja's *Photoplay Edition* bibliography lists a "bibliographic ghost" edition of this title as a book linked to the 1943 film version with Cary Grant and Raymond Massey. No such volume exists, although there is a magazine fictionization of the '43 film.) Other play tie-ins include *The Spider, Sherlock Holmes, He Who Gets Slapped, Whispering Wires, The Thirteenth Chair,* and *R.U.R (Rossum's Universal Robots)*—the work that added the word "robot" to the English language.

One unique item in the collection is a photo-illustrated book connected to a radio program: a 1930 edition of *The Hound of the Baskervilles* has a frontispiece of "Mr. Richard Gordon, the celebrated actor [shown with deerstalker hat and pipe] who plays the title role in the radio dramatization of Sherlock Holmes."

The Holmes radio series started in that year. For the first episode alone, the great William Gillette, who had originated the role onstage, played Holmes; he was immediately succeeded by Broadway actor

Richard Gordon. Except for a brief interlude in 1930-31 when Clive Brook took over, Gordon continued to play the role until 1935.[4] Radio historian Jim Harmon relates this anecdote of him:

> Fellow radio actor and coincidentally writer of some Holmes pastiche novels Frank Thomas recalls Gordon as something of a John Barrymore type. Once walking down a street at an hour far too early in the day for the actor, Gordon urgently asked Thomas, "What is that woman's name coming this way?" Thomas looked. "I don't believe I know her. Why?" Gordon shuddered. "I believe she was my third wife and I need to know how to address her if she speaks."[5]

Richard Mansfield as Jekyll and Hyde.

An additional point of interest in my particular Gordon *Hound of the Baskervilles* copy is the name of a previous owner inscribed on the flyleaf: Irene Johnson. Undoubtedly it's a coincidence, but I would still like to believe that this inscription was written by *the* Irene herself— "The Woman"—who, having eventually married some nondescript Mr. Johnson, came to treasure this very volume in her old age.

The presence of a dust jacket on a photoplay edition usually multiplies its monetary value by a factor of ten. In this collection, the rarest jacket is that for the Claude Rains *Invisible Man* volume, which is scarcer than the jackets for either *King Kong* or *Frankenstein*. The two dust wrappers that I think are the most interesting, however, are not the ones of highest monetary value. They appear on two of the *Jekyll and Hyde* volumes. The 1931 film with Fredric March generated a tie-in book whose jacket shows Jekyll/ March with an image of Hyde looking over his shoulder; but the drawing of Hyde is based not on March's makeup for this film, but on that of John Barrymore in the role from the 1920 silent version. The same image was used again for the jacket of the 1941 version with Spencer Tracy: Tracy's face is substituted for March's, but the image of Hyde is again that of the John Barrymore makeup. This linkage, I think, gives a kind of genealogical pedigree to the three best film versions of the story.

An interesting "side pocket" in photoplay collecting is a series of paperbacks published by Monarch Books in the early 1960s, which are novelizations of several contemporary horror movies. The peculiarity here is that this publisher commissioned its writers to spice up the stories with sex scenes not found in the films. All of them are very tame by today's standards, but their presence has added considerably to their prices as collectibles. Here, for instance, is one of the "hot" passages from *The Brides of Dracula*; Dr. Van Helsing, the vampire's long-time nemesis, has just rescued a young girl from a perilous situation:

> But then, taking her warm face between his hands, he tried to give her a chaste kiss. To show that he wanted her, but only under honorable conditions.
>
>   It was a useless attempt at gallantry. The girl met his mouth with her own and clutched him to her so tightly that he felt the taut nipples of her breasts pushing against his clothing. She was unconscious of her nudity, of the effect her nearness had upon him. The kiss, begun so chastely, became a frenzied joining of lips, calling up a tide of feeling within this man and woman—strangers to each other—that neither could control. Suddenly he was caressing those magnificent breasts and firm flanks and she was urging him on to greater boldness and daring. And then he was on the bed with her and their bodies united strongly in the age-old renewal of the ritual of love. As he possessed her and savored the beauty and ecstasy of her surrender, he knew that for the first time in his stormy life he was experiencing the true meaning of existence.

As a personal aside, I recall that when I first saw a copy of this book in the early '60s, when I was 14—an older friend down the street owned it—I had not yet seen any of the then-new British *Dracula* movies; and so, I remember, I had some difficulty trying to imagine Edward Van Sloan in this situation.

One of the most interesting aspects of this collection is one that, I strongly suspect, will be mirrored in any similar aggregation of old books: the volumes often contain stories other than the ones written by their authors. That is, they frequently convey interesting information about their previous owners, via handwritten inscriptions, bookplates,

Richard Gordon as Sherlock Holmes

and other markings. A number of them, for example, were inscribed as Christmas presents at some point in their pasts, including a Lon Chaney *Treasure Island*, a Bela Lugosi *Chandu the Magician* ("Frederick From Santa") and a rare "Boy Scout Edition" of *20,000 Leagues Under the Sea*. Within this collection, one copy of *Frankenstein* and a *Return of Dr. Fu Manchu* were both given as gifts on the very same date, Christmas of 1931—the former from a mother to her son ("To Bill From Mother / Christmas 1931").

The copy of *Charlie Chan Carries On* bears a cryptic handwritten note on its inside front cover, "Factual Details about London Contrasting English and Oriental Mind." (Someone, I fear, was taking those old stereotypes a bit too seriously.) Another Bela Lugosi tie-in volume, *The Deerslayer* (with photos of the actor as Chingachgook) bears an inscription, "Presented to Warren Smith for unbroken daily Bible reading October 1, 1927 to April 1, 1928."

"Coaster" rings, indicating that a wet glass or bottle once rested on the book, appear on the covers of *Baker Street*, *Bull-Dog Drummond*, and *Dracula*. *Baker Street* is a marginal book to begin with, but, for a collector, it is very hard to imagine a Bela Lugosi *Dracula* being treated so cavalierly! Some previous owner obviously did not realize how valuable this book would become—a jacketed copy was recently offered on the Internet for $2,500—and was certainly not a great fan of the old classic horror movies.

Some of the "stories" revealed by the books' physical evidences are remarkably detailed. For example, one of the Charlie Chan volumes in

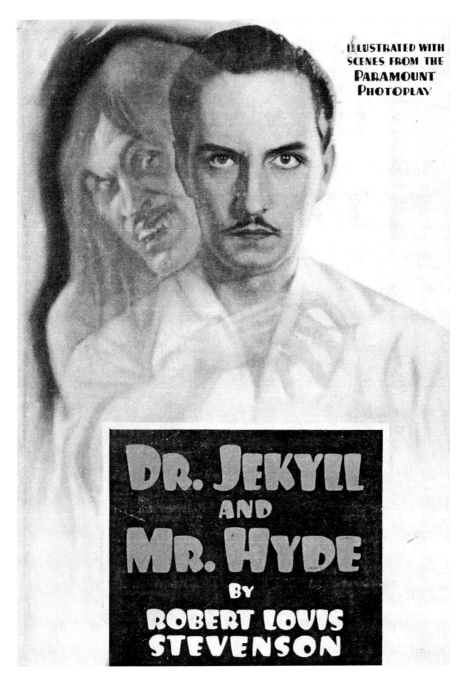

Fredric March as Jekyll

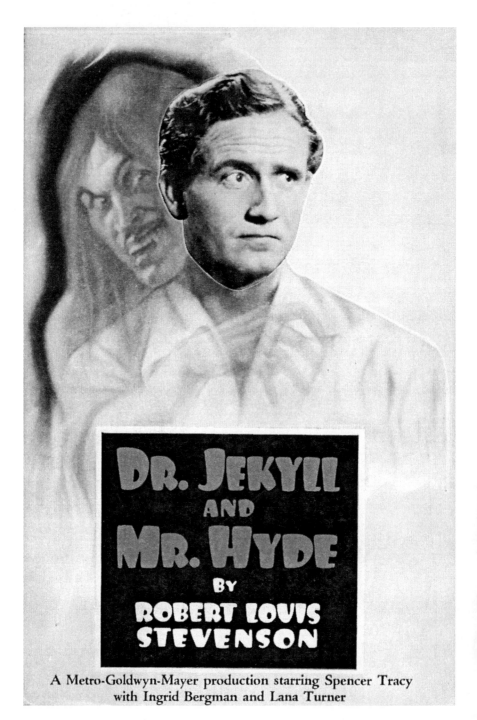

A Metro-Goldwyn-Mayer production starring Spencer Tracy
with Ingrid Bergman and Lana Turner

Spencer Tracy as Jekyll

this collection, *Behind That Curtain*, has many small bugs squashed between its pages. I therefore took it to one of the entomologists at the Smithsonian Institution, Gary F. Hevel, who is an authority on identifying insects. (He has identified over 2,200 species resident in his own back yard in Silver Spring, Maryland.[6]) Hevel identified the twenty-one microscopic creatures as midges; these are a kind of fly of the family *Chironomidae*. (Of course I was hoping the insects would turn out to be "unclassified" or "unknown to science"; unfortunately, the reality here was more prosaic.) While not confined to warm aquatic areas, midges are found especially in such locales and form a major portion of the diet of larger dragonflies. One intriguing fact is that they are attracted to light; their presence in such numbers in a book strongly suggests that they were lured by a nearby lamp.[7] This may be evidence of a good "summer read"—but one that took place by a reading lamp, near a freshwater stream or pond, rather than on a beach by an ocean shore (midges don't like salt water).

But there is evidence pointing to an even more specific situation. The inside front cover of this same volume bears a bookdealer's adhesive stamp:

> The Three
> Schuster Stores
> Book Departments
> Milwaukee

Further, a bookplate with a handwritten name, "Arthur B. Russell," is pasted on the inside front cover. This plate presents a drawing of a biplane circling a modernist, almost cubist, rendering of a cluster of skyscrapers. The book, although copyrighted in 1928, would have come out in 1929, as a photoplay edition, in conjunction with the film version of the story with Warner Baxter, E. L. Park as Chan, and Boris Karloff (in a minor role as a turbanned "Soudanese Servant"). The modernist-futurist style of the artwork and the presence of a biplane suggest that the bookplate dates to the late 1920s or early '30s, and was added when the book was brand new, or very close to the year of its publication. We may reasonably infer that Mr. Russell was the original purchaser of this volume, when it was new. (In the absence of an inscription indicating the book was presented as a gift to Mr. Russell, I will assume he purchased it himself.) In other words, if there had been another owner of the book for any length of time prior to Mr. Russell, it seems unlikely that Russell would have added, in years after the early

Markings from *Behind That Curtain* volume

1930s, a by-then-anachronistic bookplate so characteristic of the earlier time of the book's publication. It is simpler to infer that Russell added what strikes us now as a time-bound plate at the same time the book was first published—making him its probable first owner.

We may also reasonably infer that Mr. Russell kept the book for some time because the presence of a bookplate, to begin with, indicates an intention to keep the "territorially marked" volume as a permanent possession. The fact that the dust jacket was never lost also suggests a relatively stable and uncomplicated provenance, with few owners between 1929 and my acquisition of the book in the 1960s. This inference is supported by the few indications of sale or ownership transfer: beyond the original machine-stamped bookstore price of "75¢" on the dust jacket—probably the amount Mr. Russell paid—there are only two subsequent, penciled-on prices added by second-hand dealers; the first is for ".39," and the second for "5ºº," the latter being the price that I paid for the volume.

That the book was originally sold by a bookstore in Milwaukee further suggests that its initial purchaser lived in that city; so we may infer that Mr. Russell, being that likely purchaser, lived there himself in 1929 or shortly thereafter. (The later purchaser who paid ".39" is probably responsible for the book's transfer from Milwaukee to Chicago, where I acquired it.) The *Wright's Milwaukee City Directory 1930* provides confirmatory evidence. It lists three branches of the "Schuster Ed & Co" store, in the directory's classified section, under "Department Stores." It was one of their "Book Departments" that initially sold the volume to Mr. Russell. The same Milwaukee directory provides, in a column of first names lined up under the surname "Russell," the reference "Arth B r[esident] Soldiers Home." (This name does not appear in the 1929 *Directory*.) "Soldiers Home" provides a cross-reference to the "National Home for Disabled Volunteer Soldiers. Northwestern Branch," located on "National av" in Milwaukee. A fold-out map included with the volume shows the extensive grounds of the "National Soldiers Home" at that same National Avenue location. More interesting, however, is what the map also shows: a stream labeled "Menomonee River" flowing right through the middle of these grounds, and the existence of a nearby lake or pond, as well as two other ponds in the immediately adjacent Mitchell Park. A history of the Soldiers Home, *Souvenir History Northwestern Branch National Home for Disabled Volunteer Soldiers Milwaukee Wisconsin 1924*, edited by Tom L. Johnson, notes: "Through the grounds a natural brook runs," and it provides a photo of the "Lake" on the campus. An earlier history, *Souvenir of the Soldiers' Home* (Milwaukee County, Wisconsin, [1903]), provides photos of various "Barracks" buildings with wide porches on both ground and second-floor levels.

If Mr. Russell was indeed a resident of an institution for disabled veterans, his interest in books as a way to pass the time is understandable in ways not indicated simply by his bookplate. That he was an avid reader, however, is indeed indicated by the presence of that plate—only people with collections of books add such formal ownership marks to them. It is also indicated by what I think is a reasonable inference from the distribution of the insect inclusions: in the 337-page book, they appear on pages 6, 161, 180, 190, 268, 282, 285, 287, 296, 301, 303, 310, 311, 316, 325 (twice), 326, and 331, with another on one of the back-of-the-book ads and two more pressed on the inside back cover. Evidently Mr. Russell read the volume in at least three different sittings, the first and the last in outdoor environments (where the midges could come near), separated by a substantial seventy-seven page hiatus between pages 190 and 268 in which no insects at all appear. This middle session corresponds almost exactly to Chapters XII (starting on page 190) through XVI (ending on page 266).

The first sitting, at which Russell probably read Chapters I to XI, up to page 189, evidently started early in the day and then continued during the shift from daylight to twilight, at which time more midges appeared (toward the end of the session), being attracted by a reading lamp being turned on in darkening conditions. Here, however, Russell did not continue to read late into the darkness, as the insect presence, while increasing, ceases before becoming abundant.

The middle sitting, probably the next morning or afternoon, covered Chapters XII to XVI, pages 190-266 (five chapters), and took place either indoors or, more likely, in outdoor daylight—that is, without the use of a lamp in a dark environment, where it would again have attracted insects.

The third session, starting with Chapter XVII on page 267, through the end of Chapter XXII at page 337 (six chapters), was evidently done outdoors when it was already dark—probably later in the evening of that same day—next to a lamp that drew the midges almost immediately. I suspect Mr. Russell had his dinner in between the second and third sittings. This would account for the gap in the distribution of the insects. Moreover, their sudden re-appearance in much greater numbers starting with Chapter XVII indicates the time of day when the reading was resumed: an already-dark evening when a lamp had to be used right from the start. As with the first session, a porch is rather clearly indicated—the location of a favorite chair, quite probably, used in the middle session, too—since a porch would combine an outdoor environment with the proximity of an electric light.

The distribution of the insects may allow a finer inference regarding the timing of the reading periods on what were probably two successive days. Given that Mr. Russell read eleven chapters on the first day (189 pages), and that he finished them just at twilight when the midges began to be attracted to his newly turned-on light, we may infer that he started the book much earlier in the day, in the morning hours. On the second day, however, given that he finished reading the next eleven chapters (148 pages) rather late at night—in actual darkness rather than twilight—we may also infer that he started his reading later in the day, in the afternoon rather than the morning. His eagerness to finish the book despite a swarm of midges would tend to indicate a real absorption in it on that second day—a focus broken, most likely, only by dinner interruption.

The noteworthy concentration of the insects at the end of the volume suggests that Mr. Russell, sitting on that porch of the soldiers home barracks in Milwaukee on a warm evening in 1930, was indeed so very absorbed in the final chapters of the mystery story as it reached its climax and dénouement, and so greatly intent on finishing the book before he went to bed, that he would not be deterred from completing his reading even by a group of Menomonee River midges that quickly grew into a swarm about him. This disabled old soldier was, indeed, an avid reader.

Yet another book, with one of the most elaborate sets of internal markings, allows a whole story of sibling teasing to be reconstructed. One of the several *Cat and the Canary* volumes, published by Jacobsen Publishing Company in 1927, has a penciled inscription on its inside front cover, in a noticeably immature handwriting:

This book belongs to
Liz O'Brien
325 Avalon Avenue
Tonawanda, New York

Immediately below it, and in a different hand that I'll call Hand #2, is the inscription:

and
is
she
nuts!

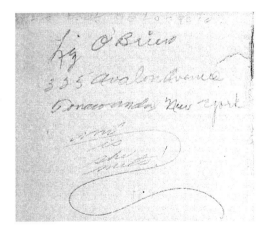

These words appear within a serpentine reverse "S" shaped squiggle; other such squig-

Markings from *The Cat and the Canary* volume.

gles, apparently meaningless, are erased below. This squiggle is not pictorially integral to the "nuts" message; it may have been inscribed by Hand #3, who frequently adds such marks.

The flyleaf bears the name "Geraldine R Hudson"; but this is crossed out in pencil. All of the other markings in the book were written either by Liz O'Brien or by one or more people teasing—or consoling—her.

The outside front cover shows a penciled squiggle similar to that on the inside front cover, but with a message in a script that I'll call Hand #3, below the book's title:

> The CAT and the CANARY [printed title]
>   are
>   nuts!
>   HA!
>   HA!
>   HA!

Also on these pages is a phrase from the popular song "Beat Me, Daddy, Eight to the Bar," written by Will Bradley. At various pages within the book are other penciled messages in the same immature Hand #3 handwriting—all but one of which have been erased. They can be read, however, with raking light. That is, light from a single point source within a darkened room, directed at the page from a very low—nearly horizontal—angle creates dark enough shadows in the furrows of the erased lines that they can be read even in the absence of the original graphite residues. These "raised" erasures suggest an interesting, if incomplete, story.

Flyleaf erasure [Hand #3]:

> Look through
>   the pages and
>   see what you
>   see
>   [squiggles]

Page 75 [Hand #3]:

> [After the opening printed line of Chapter X, "HELP! Help! Help! HELP!" an additional nine penciled exclamation points are added, and not erased.]

Page 93 erasure [Hand #3]:

> Liz loves
>   a Nigger

whose name
[?starts wi]th
[?Ge]orge

Page 118 [Hand #3]:

[The last line of Chapter XIV reads, "The world went black before
Paul's eyes." A penciled line is drawn below it, followed by the
unerased handwritten mimicry:]

The world went
Black before Paul's
eyes.
[The handwritten "B" is capitalized.]

Pages 128-29 erasures [Hand #3]:

!!Jiggers! Jiggers! Cops
and niggers!!!!!!!!
[squiggle]
That's
[For] [? illegible erasure]
you,
crazy!
nuts to the person
who reads this
book!!!!!!!!!!
including R. K.
[squiggles]

Inside back cover [Liz's handwriting]:

This Book belongs to:
Liz O'Brien
325 Avalon Avenue
Tonawanda, New York
[several underscores tapered to form an inverted pyramid]

Immediately below the ownership inscription is another penciled
note in what I'll call Hand #4:

A darn
swell
kid
x o
By R K

Back cover:

[penciled squiggle, probably Hand #3]

Since the book belonged to young Miss Liz O'Brien, who wrote her name and address in it twice, I'm guessing that it was another two young people (Hands #2 and #3), close enough to her to have had access to her possessions while she was absent, who defaced the book. The main defacer's handwriting (#3) is noticeably immature. Annoying brothers strike me as likely candidates for Hands #2 and #3. The "R K" of Hand #4, in contrast, offers consoling words ("A darn swell Kid" and a kiss "x" and hug "o") to Liz; perhaps we have an older sibling here. It is noteworthy that Hand #3 aims some of his [?] teasing at R. K. ("nuts to the person who reads this book ... including R. K."), who was evidently known to be sympathetic to young Liz. A tight social grouping is suggested in that not only did Hands #2 and #3 have access to Liz's personal possession, to write in it, but so did Hand #4, of "R. K." A family group seems plausible.

The teasing centers around the "n" word and is emphasized by the writer's copying in pencil the printed sentence from the novel, "The world went Black before Paul's eyes," and capitalizing the "B." A musical phrase from "Beat Me, Daddy, Eight to the Bar" appears twice. A best-selling recording of this popular song was issued in 1940.[8] This provides a rough date for the defacers' writings. Since the ink-written name "Geraldine R. Hudson" on the flyleaf is crossed out in pencil, it is reasonable to infer that she was a previous owner of the book, before Miss O'Brien. (The book was published in 1927; if the O'Brien period dates to the time of the song, around 1940, there would have been ample time for a previous possession.) In the final analysis, one can only guess about an interracial childhood friendship that ran into the prejudices of the early 1940s.[9] In any event, young Miss O'Brien tried to erase most of the remarks of her main teaser, Hand #3.

In an attempt to gain more information about this book, I wrote to everyone named "O'Brien" in the current telephone directory for Tonawanda, New York, and sent photocopies of the title page and of the girl's handwritten address on the inside front cover. I did not mention the "n" word in my letters; I simply asked if the recipients might know anything about this Liz O'Brien or "R. K." Even with self-addressed, stamped envelopes included with my letters, I received no replies at all. (My imagination has now magnified Tonawanda, N.Y., into a kind of "Stephen King" town, possessing a horrible shared secret, that an outsider dare not show up to investigate.) In any event, as Kipling wrote, "There the matter rests."

Other volumes in the collection also suggest at least "mini-stories":

- The copy of *The Miracle Man* seems to have been read by at least two people: one turned down corners, at an average space of about 27 pages apart; the other reader *tore off corners* averaging about 21 pages apart. The more barbaric of the two evidently had a shorter attention span. (Somehow this is not surprising.) The story is 300 pages long; the last bent corner appears at page 251, but the last torn corner is at 195—perhaps the tearer couldn't even finish the book. The cover of the volume is unusually smudged and dirtied, and numerous indications of dirty fingers, and stained corners turned by licked fingers, show up throughout—not just before page 195. This book was not well-treated by any of its readers.
- One of the *Bull-Dog Drummond* volumes bears an inscription on its inside front cover: "This book is the property of / Emery J. Kelley / Please return." One of my copies of *Raffles* bears a signature in ink of "Donald Storm"; added in pencil, subsequently, are the notes:

> Property of 'Al' G. Wiederer
> 717 Aldine Ave.
> Chicago, Illinois

followed by:

> Receiver of the
> Don Storm Estate.

Mr. Wiederer has added two further notes to the inside front cover:

> Rental—
> 5¢ per Week
> 1¢ a day over

and

> Special Rates
> to Friends!

Evidently he received at least a couple nickels: this volume, too, shows turned down page corners. At least two readers seem to be indicated, however, since some of the bent corners appear quite close to each other (pp. 61 and 63, 76 and 79), suggesting two readers who reached nearly the same pages on separate occasions—that is, it appears unlikely that a single reader would get as far as page 61 and stop, and then stop again at page 63; similarly for pages 76 and 79. A reinforcement for this inference is that the corner-bends at 61 and 76 are made at noticeably different angles from those at 63 and 79.

- Sometimes the clues are both numerous and tantalizing—but, still, they don't add up to much. One of my copies of *Seven Keys to Baldpate* has unusual markings. The inscription "David . H. Hodges / Feb 14. 1926" appears in beautifully, even ornamentally, written pencil script on the inside front cover. This date puts the signature in the same year as the book's publication; it came out as a tie-in to the 1926 Paramount film version. Evidently Mr. Hodges acquired the book when it was brand new. A few inches below his inscription, and written in ink by a different adult hand, is the single word "Suburban"— inscribed upside down(!). Many pages throughout the book show what seem to be random scribble marks made by a child; those on the title page, however, are a bit more formal, showing two penciled arrows and a carefully blocked-off area, nearly rectangular, of filled-in penciling. The initials "A / M.B" appear above it. The book shows finger smudges, even reasonably distinct fingerprints, in margins throughout. The binding is unusually battered, too. I can only surmise that the rough treatment afforded this volume came only after it left the possession of the refined Mr. Hodges.
- The copy of *The Mysterious Island* has a name and address inscribed, in a young person's hand, on its half-title page: "Richard Bannon / 831 West 50 Place / Chicago Ill." All three lines are written in pencil, but the first two have been carefully traced over in ink. Below the inscription is a pasted-on gold star. Perhaps young Master Bannon was given the star as a reward in school for having read, all the way through, this 500-page book. His pride of accomplishment may have been the occasion that induced him then to re-inscribe his name and address in a more permanent form.
- *Arsenic and Old Lace* evidently went through the personal ownership of several people in the same family. Its flyleaf is embossed with the name "A. W. Martin Marino, M. D. / Eighty Hanson Place / Brooklyn, N.Y." On the inside front cover, however, the inscription "Doris Marino April / 1941" appears, with "Doris" written over an erasure, possibly spelling "Mr. Martin." At some point the book passed to a son, who evidently assumed the worst about potential borrowers: his note on the back inside cover reads, simply, "Stolen from Martin Marino, Jr." (It is possible that Doris could have been junior's sister rather than mother.) Most curious, however, is a coin-size, circular penciled drawing, intermediate in size between a nickel and a quarter, that appears on the inside front cover. It shows the handwritten motto of "In God We Trust" and the left-facing profile of a man with

long, tied hair, comparable to the images of Thomas Jefferson or George Washington on their coins. The profile of this individual, however, is unmistakably that of Boris Karloff, who starred in the stage production of *Arsenic and Old Lace*, and who appears in two of the photo illustrations in this volume.

Markings from *Arsenic and Old Lace* volume

Was Martin Marino, Jr., a particular fan of Karloff? Did he and some of his family come in from Brooklyn to attend a Broadway performance of the play in which Karloff appeared? Was a particular interest in Karloff his reason for signaling to all others that any removal of the book from his possession was unwelcome? (As a fan of Karloff myself, that's just how I feel about my own current possession of the same book.) Was this interest in the actor, evidenced in the drawing, the reason that either Martin Marino, Sr., or Doris transferred ownership of the book to Martin, Jr., in the first place? It seems less likely that the father or Doris, rather than junior himself, would mark up the book by drawing a caricature of Boris Karloff in it while it was in their own possession. In any event, something made Martin, Jr.'s, attachment to this volume strong enough to be indicated explicitly to other potential readers ("Stolen from"), whereas there is evidence that two other owners in the same family put the boy's interest in the book above any desire they may have had to retain possession of it themselves. The evidence here speaks well of the older Marinos' encouragement of their younger family member's interest in books and reading.

- The *Master Mystery* volume in this collection, tied to a 1919 Houdini serial, bears the inky finger and hand prints of a small child on its back cover. The same volume shows extreme fading of the binding at the very top and bottom edges of its spine; the rest of the spine and cover is in comparatively good, unfaded shape. Evidently the book was once protected by a dust jacket while resting for years on a shelf that received direct sunlight, which bleached the edges unprotected by the jacket. The child-prints must have come later, when the jacket was lost—or perhaps its owner removed the jacket while reading the book, at which time his or her child discovered the volume. Two water stains also appear at the base of the spine, but do not wrap around to spot either cover; these evidently splashed onto the book while it was tightly shelved between other volumes, at a time subsequent to the loss of its dust jacket. Although there are no names or inscriptions written anywhere in this copy, all of this suggests the likelihood of at least two different previous owners, and very different shelving conditions.

These volumes, in short, present not just the stories of their authors, but those of their owners as well. Indications of rewards for young people's reading accomplishments, or of retirement enthusiasm, racial tensions, youthful entrepreneurial schemes, intergenerational family dynamics, personal habits (licking fingers to turn pages, bending or tearing page corners, shelving customs, using books as coasters)—all such details open up glimpses of interesting life incidents stored in these old books like memorabilia forgotten in musty attic trunks. Such meditations make one wonder how many other stories, perhaps embedded in some of the other markings by previous owners, are now beyond the possibility of any similar reconstructions. The several books inscribed as Christmas presents in decades long gone, I think, provide particularly tantalizing residues of rich experiences; but they are now only faint fragrances of what, possibly, were whole ranges of emotional associations that may once have richly enveloped these volumes.

I will not belabor the reader with the multiple and varied associations that I have come to attach, myself, to many of the quaint and curious volumes of forgotten lore contained in this collection. As a concluding thought, however, I will beg the reader's indulgence to single out but one: that, long ago, a few of the more unlikely titles recorded here served to hook me into the joys, not only of collecting, but of reading itself. Michael Dirda, the Pulitzer Prize winning critic, once wrote wistfully of one of his sons, "He had entered the Golden Age—roughly 10 to 15—when printed matter becomes more real to us than at any other time of our lives, when no hours are so blessed as those spent alone with a book."[10] These volumes did much to usher me into that wondrous initial experience of reading, at a comparable period of my own life. As I've grown older, of course, I've come to see them through a

Hazlittian "magnifying glass" of awarenesses not accessible to my younger self; but I've also found that the same books have retained a power to tunnel through time. Indeed, reading them today enables even a bifocled pair of eyes to recapture directly more than a few cherished glimpses of that innocent and joyous Golden Age.

Notes

1. One is reminded here of the Sherlock Holmes story "The Problem of Thor Bridge," in which Watson tantalizingly mentions an "unfinished tale" concerning "Isadora Persano, the well-known journalist and duelist, who was found stark raving mad with a match box in front of him which contained a remarkable worm said to be unknown to science." Perhaps Mr. Persano was the victim of another of the entomological horrors of Dr. Fu Manchu. One also wonders, however, why Fu could not simply have shot his enemies, or stabbed them; but then, probably, he would never have gained his reputation as an "evil genius" if he had been that unimaginative in *modus operandi*. The volume in which this "Zayat Kiss" passage appears is all the more interesting because, in the movie from which it reproduces photographs, Warner Oland plays the Oriental villain—the same actor who, a few years later, would become much more famous as an Oriental hero, the great detective Charlie Chan.

2. Compare these passages to the treatment of a similar situation by a much better writer, Arthur Conan Doyle. Compound-complex sentence structures, frequent use of simile and metaphor, a rich variety of telling details, and appeals to several senses all grace the opening of Chapter IV of *The Sign of the Four*:

> We followed the Indian down a sordid and common passage, ill-lit and worse furnished, until he came to a door upon the right, which he threw open. A blaze of yellow light streamed out upon us, and in the center of the glare there stood a small man with a very high head, a bristle of red hair all round the fringe of it, and a bald, shining scalp which shot out from among it like a mountain-peak from fir-trees. He writhed his hands together as he stood, and his features were in a perpetual jerk—now smiling, now scowling, but never for an instant in repose. Nature had given him a pendulous lip, and a too visible line of yellow and irregular teeth, which he strove feebly to conceal by constantly passing his hand over the lower part of his face. In spite of his obtrusive baldness, he gave the impression of youth. In point of fact, he had just turned his thirtieth year.
>
> "Your sevant, Miss Morstan," he kept repeating, in a thin, high voice. "Your servant, gentlemen. Pray step into my little sanctum. A small place, Miss Morstan, but furnished to my own liking. An oasis of art in the howling desert of South London."
>
> We were all astonished by the appearance of the apartment into which he invited us. In that sorry house it looked as out-of-place as a diamond of the first water in a setting of brass. The richest and glossiest of curtains and tapestries draped the walls, looped back here and there to expose some richly-mounted painting or Oriental vase. The carpet was of amber and black, so soft and so thick that the foot sank pleasantly into it, as into a bed of moss. Two great tiger-skins thrown athwart it increased the suggestion of Eastern

luxury, as did a huge hookah which stood upon a mat in the corner. A lamp in the fashion of a silver dove was hung from an almost invisible golden wire in the center of the room. As it burned it filled the air with a subtle and aromatic odor.

3. See C. Alex Pinkson, Jr., "The Stage Premiere of *Dr. Jekyll and Mr. Hyde*," *Nineteenth Century Theatre Research*, 14, 1 & 2 (1986), 21–43. Pinkston also mentions that the double-exposure picture is the "only surviving photograph of Mansfield as Jekyll and Hyde" (p. 28).

4. Jim Harmon, *Radio Mystery and Adventure and Its Appearances in Film, Television and Other Media* (Jefferson, North Carolina: McFarland, 1992), 171.

5. *Ibid.*, 171.

6. Fern Shen, "Mister Bug," *The Washington Post* (October 9, 2001), C16.

7. One of my other photoplay editions, Mrs. Belloc Lowndes's *The House of Peril*, contains an interesting relevant passage:

> Sylvia sat down by the open window.
> "You need not light a candle, Anna," she said. "It's so pleasant just now; so quiet and cool; and the light would only attract those horrid midges. They seem to me the only things I have to find fault with in Lacville" [p. 107].

8. *Popular Music, 1920–1979. A Revised Cumulation*, edited by Nat Shapiro and Bruce Pollock (Detroit, Michigan: Gale Research Company, 1985), p. 195.

9. John W. Percy, in *Growing Pains: Kenmore-Tonawanda Comes of Age* (Kenmore, N.Y.: Partners' Press, 1986), recounts details of a Ku Klux Klan meeting in the Tonawanda area in 1924. James Bilotta's "Life in the Greater Buffalo Area, 1930s–1960s," *Afro-Americans in New York Life and History*, 13, 2 (July, 1989), 47–55, recounts the recollections of a lifelong black resident of the same area: "Mr. Brown remembers that [in the 1930s] while white children seemed somewhat colorblind and were willing to mingle and play with him, their parents were usually opposed to this 'mixing.' On one occasion a white mother snatched her child away, simply because she didn't want him talking to a black child" (p. 48).

10. Michael Dirda, "Readings," *The Washington Post Book World* (May 13, 2001), 15.

THE CATALOG

"Abbott & Costello Meet Frankenstein." In: *Movie Story Magazine*, Vol. 25, No. 171 (July 1948), 52–53, 84–86.

One photo (pp. 52–53) of Abbott and Costello standing over Glenn Strange, as the Monster, resting in a packing case. Cover says *Movie Story*; contents page says *Movie Story Magazine*.

The Abominable Dr. Phibes see *Dr. Phibes*

About the Murder of the Circus Queen. By Anthony Abbot. New York: Grosset & Dunlap, 1932.

Front and back endpapers have 16 photos from Columbia's *The Circus Queen Murder* with Adolphe Menjou as Thatcher Colt.

About the Murder of the Night Club Lady. By Anthony Abbot. New York: Grosset & Dunlap, 1931.

Four photos from the Columbia film *Night Club Lady* with Adolphe Menjou as Thatcher Colt. Dust jacket has colored picture of Menjou.

The Adventures of Kathlyn. By Harold MacGrath. Indianapolis: The Bobbs-Merrill Company Publishers, c. 1914.

The *American Film Institute Catalog/Feature Films 1911–1920* says, "*The Adventures of Kathlyn* is considered by film historians to be the first motion picture serial as distinguished from films released in a series." A twenty-seven reel version was released beginning December 29, 1913; it was re-edited into a ten reel version released in 1916. Eight b&w photos appear in this volume. Photocopied dust jacket has color photo/artwork from the film on front, and color silhouette on back, of "Kathlyn W. Williams in the famous motion picture play The Adventures of Kathlyn by Harold Mac Grath".

The Adventures of Sherlock Holmes. By A. Conan Doyle. New York: A. L. Burt Company, c. 1892, 1920.

Dust jacket (only) has a photo of Clive Brook, on both the front cover and the spine, from the 1932 Fox Picture *Sherlock Holmes*.

The Adventures of Sherlock Holmes. By Sir Arthur Conan Doyle; adapted by Olive Eckerson; edited by Wallace R. Murray. New York: Globe Book Company, 1950.

Children's school text illustrated with twelve photos from the Basil Rathbone film *Adventures of Sherlock Holmes*, plus one photo of William Gillette as Holmes, three of Conan Doyle, one of Doyle's study. Cover has drawing of Holmes, roughly based on Rathbone.

The Adventures of Sherlock Holmes see "Sherlock Holmes"

"After the Thin Man." Story by James Reid. In: *Romantic Movie Stories*, Vol. 7, No. 34 (February 1937), 28–31, 65–67.
   Nine photos from the MGM picture with William Powell, Myrna Loy, and James Stewart. The story is told indirectly; the ending of the mystery is not revealed. Credits on page 29; additional photos of Powell and Loy in table of contents, page 5, and on cover.

"After the Thin Man." In: *Screen Romances*, Vol. 16, No. 93 (February, 1937), 83–96, 98, 122.
   No author credit given for the "Complete Book-Length Novel." Color cover plus twelve photos from the MGM film with William Powell, Myrna Loy, and James Stewart. George Zucco is listed as "George Cucco" in the credits on page 85. (The same issue has "The Mandarin Mystery.")

The Agony Column see *The Second Floor Mystery*

And Then There Were None. By Agatha Christie. New York: Grosset & Dunlap, 1945.
   Six photos from 1945 Fox movie on three double-sided pages, plus double-page photo spreads at title page and endpapers. Dust jacket has additional b&w photos on front and spine.

The Animal World. Dell comic No. 713. New York: Dell Publishing Co., Inc., 1956.
   Comic book version of the 1956 Warner Bros. film. Front cover has color artwork of tyrannosaurus and triceratops. Inside front cover has seven b&w photos of the same two animals fighting, and film credits. Special effects by Ray Harryhausen.

"Another Thin Man." In: *Boy's Cinema*, No. 1065 (May 11, 1940), 8–14, 19–20.
   "Nick Charles, his wife Nora, their baby and Asta, the terrier, go for a quiet week-end to a lonely house, and become involved in a baffling crime mystery." Cover plus ten internal photos from 1939 MGM film with William Powell, Myrna Loy, Virginia Grey, C. Aubrey Smith, Nat Pendleton, Patric Knowles, and Sheldon Leonard. Credits on page 20.

Arsene Lupin. By Edgar Jepson and Maurice Leblanc. London: George Newnes, Limited, n.d.

Paperback. Front cover has one b&w photo of Lionel and John Barrymore from 1932 MGM film, their first together.

"Arsene Lupin." Fictionized by Ethel M. Pomeroy. In: *Screen Romances*, Vol. 6, No. 35 (April 1932), 10–17, 90, 92–93.
Nine photos from the MGM film with John and Lionel Barrymore, Karen Morley, John Miljan, and Tully Marshall. (The same issue has "Tarzan.")

Arsene Lupin see *The Teeth of the Tiger*

"Arsene Lupin Returns." In: *Movie Story Magazine*, Vol. 10, No. 48 (April, 1938), 36–37, 42, 44–48.
Three photos from the MGM film with Melvyn Douglas as the master French thief Arsene Lupin, who, in retirement, has adopted the name Rene Farrand; an additional small photo appears with the table of contents on page 5. Warren William, George Zucco, Virginia Bruce, Nat Pendleton, and E. E. Clive also appear. (Douglas and William both played the Lone Wolf in other films.)

Arsenic and Old Lace. A Comedy by Joseph Kesserling. New York: Random House, 1941.
Script of the Broadway play, with original cast list from January 10, 1941. Four glossy photos bound in, two showing Boris Karloff in the role of Jonathan Brewster.

"Arsenic and Old Lace." In: *Movie Story Magazine*, Vol. 18, No. 127 (November 1944), 34–37, 84–90.
Four photos from Frank Capra's Warner Bros. picture with Cary Grant, Raymond Massey, and Peter Lorre.

At the Earth's Core. By Edgar Rice Burroughs. Garden City, N.Y.: Nelson Doubleday, Inc., c. 1914.
Book club edition with eight photos from 1976 American-International/Amicus film with Doug McClure and Peter Cushing. Dust jacket has colored montage drawing of scenes from the movie.

Background to Danger. By Eric Ambler. New York: Triangle Books, 1943.
Dust jacket has one photo of Peter Lorre holding a gun on Brenda Marshall and George Raft, from the 1943 Warner Bros. film.

Backstage Phantom see *The Last Warning*

Baker Street: A Musical Adventure of Sherlock Holmes. Book by Jerome Coopersmith. Music and lyrics by Marian Grudeff and Raymond Jessel. Garden City, N.Y.: Doubleday & Company, Inc., 1966.
Eight photos from the Broadway production.

The Bat. By Mary Roberts Rinehart. London: A WDL Book; World Distributors, 1960. No. M952.
Front cover has color artwork with tie-in note to "An Allied Artists Picture—Distributed by Warner-Pathé / Starring: Vincent Price—Agnes Moorehead."

The Bat [comic book]. Inside cover: *Mary Roberts Rinehart's The Bat,* No. 1 (of 1), August 1992. Westlake Village, Calif.: Adventure Comics, 1992.
Association item; not a photoplay. B&w (except for front cover) comic format using characters' names from Rinehart-Hopwood story but radically changing plot so that everyone is killed (by evil twin, in Bat costume, of Cornelia Van Gorder, who is portrayed as young, paranoid, and greedy).

The Bat: A Mystery Story. By Mary Roberts Rinehart and Avery Hopwood. New York: George H. Doran Company, c. 1926. Title page reads: *The Bat: A Novel From the Play by Mary Roberts Rinehart and Avery Hopwood.*
Dust jacket (only) has colored photo from the 1926 United Artists movie with Jack Pickford and Louise Fazenda, "Courtesy of Roland West."

The Bat: A Play of Mystery in Three Acts. By Mary Roberts Rinehart and Avery Hopwood. New York: Samuel French, c. 1920, c. 1932 (Acting Version).
Play script with four photographs from the New York stage production; two show empty sets, two show cast members in character. Scene design sketches are also included, as is a section of press releases to garner "Publicity Through Your Local Papers." Page 4 gives credits of the first performance of the play as produced at the Morosco Theatre in New York.

The Bat Whispers: Photoplay Title for "The Bat." By Mary Roberts Rinehart and Avery Hopwood. New York: Grosset & Dunlap, c. 1926. (Title page reads: *The Bat: A Novel From the Play by Mary Roberts Rinehart and Avery Hopwood.*)
Dust jacket (only) has green-tinted drawing of Chester Morris from the 1930 United Artists movie. This is the same book as that for the 1926 film (above); only the dust jacket is different.

The Bat Whispers: Photoplay Title for "The Bat." By Mary Roberts Rine-
    hart and Avery Hopwood. New York: Grosset & Dunlap, c. 1926. Title
    page reads: *The Bat: Movie Title The Bat Whispers ...* with illustrations
    from Roland West's Production for United Artists Starring Chester
    Morris.
    Eight b&w photos from the 1930 United Artists movie are bound in.
The dust jacket is identical to the above, with a green-tinted drawing of
Chester Morris from movie. The title page is different from the two copies
above.

"The Beast with Five Fingers." In: *Movie Story Magazine*, Vol. 22, No. 154
    (February 1947), 48–49, 90, 92–94, 96.
    Two photos from the Warner Bros. Picture with Robert Alda, Andrea
King, Peter Lorre, and J. Carroll Naish. A third photo appears in a side-
bar article, "On the Set of *The Beast with Five Fingers*," on page 90.

The Beast With Five Fingers: Twenty Tales of the Uncanny. By William Fryer
    Harvey. New York: E. P. Dutton & Company, Inc., 1947.
    Back cover of dust jacket (only) has four photos from the Warner Bros.
picture with Robert Alda, Andrea King, and Peter Lorre.

"Bedlam." Fictionized by Susan Conrad. In: *Screen Romances*, Vol. 28, No.
    200 (January 1946), 42–45, 76–77.
    Five photos from the RKO-Radio Picture with Boris Karloff.

Behind That Curtain. By Earl Derr Biggers. New York: Grosset & Dun-
    lap, c. 1928.
    Four photos from the 1929 Fox movie with E. L. Park as Chan. Dust
jacket has drawing of Chan unrelated to the movie. Park/Chan appears in
photo opposite page 254. Boris Karloff played a Soudanese servant in this
film, but his picture does not appear in this book. Back cover of dust jacket
has photo of Biggers.

"Behind the Mask." In: *Boy's Cinema*, No. 653 (June 18, 1932), 3–10, 26–27.
    "For over a year the American Secret Service had been on the trail of
a gang of drug traffickers, but the identity of Mr. X remained a sinister
mystery which daring men died to fathom. A thriller of thrillers with a
terrific climax." Cover plus eight internal photos from the 1932 Columbia film with Edward Van Sloan as a mad doctor, and Boris Karloff.
(Karloff appears in three pictures.) Although filmed before *Frankenstein*,
it was not released until immediately afterwards. Film credits given on
page 2.

The Benson Murder Case. By S. S. Van Dine. New York: A. L. Burt Company, c. 1921.

Four photos from the 1930 Paramount film with William Powell; extra colored picture of Powell appears on dust jacket.

Best Mystery and Suspense Plays of the Modern Theatre. With Prefaces and Introductory Note by Stanley Richards. New York: Dodd, Mead & Company, 1971.

Anthology of ten plays with photos from their stage productions: *Witness for the Prosecution* by Agatha Christie; *Sleuth* by Anthony Shaffer; *Child's Play* by Robert Marasco; *Angel Street* by Patrick Hamilton; *Dangerous Corner* by J. B. Priestley; *Dracula* by Hamilton Deane and John L. Balderston (Lugosi photo from screen version); *Dial "M" for Murder* by Frederick Knott; *The Letter* by W. Somerset Maugham; *Arsenic and Old Lace* by Joseph Kesserling (photo with Boris Karloff); and *Bad Seed* by Maxwell Anderson.

"Beyond Shanghai." In: *Boy's Cinema*, No. 808 (June 8, 1935), 13–16, 27–28.

"For 600 years the mystery of the city of Angkor was lost to the world. Then two French explorers set out to find it, and were beset with the jealous fury of an age-old ape-god. A magnificent adventure in the jungles of Indo-China, featuring the explorers themselves—Gene Hue and Francois Descartes." Four photos, two of someone in an ape costume, from the Wardour Films, Ltd., production.

The Big Clock. By Kenneth Fearing. New York: Harcourt, Brace and Company, c. 1946.

Dust jacket has one photo of Ray Milland and Maureen O'Sullivan from the Paramount picture.

The Big Sleep. By Raymond Chandler. Cleveland and New York: The World Publishing Company, 1946.

Frontispiece, three double-sided pages, endpapers with photos from the 1946 Warner Bros. film with Humphrey Bogart. Dust jacket has eight photos.

"The Big Sleep." Fictionized by David Frazer. In: *Screen Romances*, Vol. 28, No. 209 (October 1946), 43–44, 102–108.

Seven photos from the Warner Bros. film with Humphrey Bogart and Lauren Bacall.

The Bishop Murder Case. By S. S. Van Dine. New York: Grosset & Dunlap, c. 1929.

Four photos from the 1930 MGM film with Basil Rathbone as Philo

Vance. Dust jacket has three more photos on back cover; front is color drawing of a skeletal hand holding a chess piece.

The Bishop Murder Case. By S. S. Van Dine. With a new introduction by Chris Steinbrunner. Boston, Mass.: Gregg Press, 1980 reprint, 1929 edition.
  Five photos from the 1930 MGM film with Basil Rathbone as Philo Vance.

"The Bishop Murder Case." By Val Lewton. In: *Moving Picture Stories*, Vol. 36, No. 841 (February 18, 1930), 12–14, 22, 25–26 [part 1]; Vol. 36, No. 842 (March 4, 1930), 21–22, 29–30, 32 [part 2].
  Part 1 has two photos from the MGM screen version with Basil Rathbone as Philo Vance, and Roland Young. Part 2 has one photo. (The No. 842 issue also has Part 1 of "Murder on the Roof.")

The Black Camel. By Earl Derr Biggers. New York: Grosset & Dunlap, c. 1929.
  Four photos from the 1931 Fox Movietone film with Warner Oland, Bela Lugosi, Dwight Frye, Robert Young, Mary Gordon. Three show Lugosi; of them, one shows Oland, Lugosi, and Frye together. (This is the earliest surviving Chan film with Oland in the role; his earlier *Charlie Chan Carries On* is a lost film; it is also the first film Lugosi made after *Dracula*.)

"The Black Cat." Fictionized by Herbert Westen. In: *Romantic Movie Stories*, Vol. 1, No. 9 (July 1934), 38–41, 70–72.
  Four photos from the 1934 Universal film with Boris Karloff, Bela Lugosi, David Manners, and Jaqueline Wells.

"The Black Cat." In: *Movie Story Magazine*, Vol. 16, No. 86 (June 1941), 42–43, 75–81.
  Five photos from the 1941 Universal picture, showing Bela Lugosi, Basil Rathbone, Broderick Crawford, Gale Sondergaard, Anne Gwynne, and Alan Ladd.

"Black Friday." Original story by Sam Robbins. In: *Movie Story Magazine*, 14, 74 (June 1940), 48–50, 52, 54–57.
  Ten photos from the 1940 Universal film with Karloff, Lugosi, Stanley Ridges, Anne Nagel, and Anne Gwynne. An additional photo of Karloff appears in the table of contents, page 5.

"The Black Room." Fictionized by Beverly Floyd. In: *Romantic Movie Stories*, 3, 18 (September 1935), 43–45, 56, 58–59, 61.

Five photos from the Columbia picture; all five show Karloff as either Gregor or Anton (dual role).

"The Black Room." In: *Boy's Cinema*, No. 842 (February 1, 1936), 3–12, 25–26.
"Because of a legend in the De Berghman family to the effect that, when twins were born, one will kill the other, a room in which murder has been done is bricked up after the birth of Gregor and Anton. But Gregor grows up to become a fiendish tyrant—and the Black Room takes its toll." Ten photos (including front cover) from the 1936 Columbia Pictures film with Boris Karloff in a dual role. Credits on page 28 list Edward Van Sloan in a small role.

The Blackbird see *The Mocking Bird*

"A Blind Bargain." Adapted from the photoplay by Ethel Rosemon. In: *Moving Picture Stories*, Vol. 21, No. 525 (January 19, 1923), 1–4, 23.
Two photos from the 1923 Goldwyn film show Lon Chaney as Dr. Lamb and as The Hunchback.

"The Blue Dahlia." In: *Movie Story Magazine*, Vol. 21, No. 146 (June 1946), 38–39, 104.
Two photos, of Alan Ladd and Veronica Lake, from the Paramount Picture written by Raymond Chandler. (The same issue has "Dressed to Kill.")

The Blue Dahlia: A Screenplay. By Raymond Chandler; edited with an Afterword by Matthew J. Bruccoli. Paperback. Carbondale and Edwardsville, Ill.: Southern Illinois University Press, 1976.
Script from the 1946 Paramount picture with Alan Ladd and Veronica Lake, illustrated internally with seven glossy b&w lobby poster cards, framed in blue margins, and full color poster on dust jacket. Frontispiece is photo of Raymond Chandler.

Boston Blackie. By Jack Boyle. With a new introduction by Edward D. Hoch. Boston, Mass.: Gregg Press, 1979.
Reprint of the 1919 edition illustrated with twelve photos from various Boston Blackie movies.

Boy's Cinema—"Another Thin Man," "Behind the Mask" (Van Sloan, Karloff), "Beyond Shanghai," "The Black Room," "Bulldog Drummond in Africa," "Bulldog Drummond's Bride," "Bulldog Drummond's Peril," "Calling Philo Vance," "The Case of the Black Cat," "The Cat Creeps,"

"The Circus Shadow," "Dr. Jekyll and Mr. Hyde" (March), "A Face in the Fog," "Flash Gordon," "The Gracie Allen Murder Case," "The House of Mystery," "The Kennel Murder Case," "The Last Days of Pompeii," "The Laurel-Hardy Murder Mystery," "The Lone Wolf Returns," "The Mark of the Vampire," "Midnight Phantom," "The Million Dollar Mystery," "The Miracle Man" (Morris), "The Mummy," "Murder on a Bridle Path," "Murder on a Honeymoon," "The Mystery of Edwin Drood," "Nick Carter—Master Detective," "The Perils of Pauline," "Postal Inspector," "The Raven," "The River House Mystery," "The Rogues' Tavern," "S.O.S. Coast Guard," "The Secret of the Chateau," "A Shot in the Dark," "The Spanish Cape Mystery," "The Thin Man," "Think Fast, Mr. Moto," "Ticket to a Crime," "To-morrow at Seven," "Vanishing Shadow," and "The Werewolf of London."

The Brasher Doubloon. By Raymond Chandler. Cleveland and New York: The World Publishing Company, 1946.
   Dust jacket has seven photos from the 1947 20th Century–Fox film with George Montgomery and Nancy Guild.

"The Bride of Frankenstein." Fictionized by Mary Chadbourne-Brown. In: *Screen Romances* (May 1935), 84–87, 110.
   Four photos on green-tinted paper, showing Karloff (twice), Colin Clive, Ernest Thesiger, Valerie Hobson, and Una O'Connor in scenes from the Universal film.

Bride of Frankenstein. By Carl Dreadstone. Adapted from the screenplay by William Hurlbut. With an introduction by Ramsey Campbell. New York: Berkley Publishing Corporation, 1977.
   Numerous photos from the 1935 Universal movie.

The Brides of Dracula. By Dean Owen. Based on an original screenplay by Jimmy Sangster. Derby, Connecticut: Monarch Books, Inc., 1960. No. MM602.
   Front cover has color artwork of Dracula holding a woman; back cover has the same drawing tinted green. No photos in this tie-in with the 1960 Hammer film.

The Broadway Murders: Photoplay Title Murder on the Roof see *Murder on the Roof*

Bull-Dog Drummond. By Cyril McNeile. New York: Grosset & Dunlap, c. 1919, 1920.

Four photos from the stage play as produced by Charles Dillingham with A. E. Matthews as Drummond.

Bull-Dog Drummond. By Cyril McNeile. New York: Grosset & Dunlap, c. 1919, 1920.
Four photos from the 1929 United Artists film with Ronald Colman and Loretta Young.

"Bulldog Drummond Escapes." Fictionized by A. R. Goldin. In: *Screen Romances,* Vol. 16, No. 94 (March 1937), 42–45, 117–20.
Seven photos from the Paramount picture with Ray Milland, Heather Angel, and Reginald Denny.

"Bulldog Drummond in Africa." In: *Boy's Cinema,* No. 999 (February 4, 1939), 17–21.
"A thrilling tale of the famous adventurer, in which he fights a gang of spies seeking to gain possession of a secret radio wave." Four photos from the Paramount Picture with John Howard, Heather Angel, and J. Carroll Naish. Credits given on page 27.

Bulldog Drummond Strikes Back. By H. C. McNeile. New York: Grosset & Dunlap, c. 1933.
Endpapers have sixteen photos from the 1934 United Artists film with Ronald Colman; dust jacket has additional color artwork of Colman and Loretta Young on front, b&w artwork of Warner Oland on spine. Oland appears in three of the photos.

"Bulldog Drummond Strikes Back." From the screenplay by Nunnally Johnson. Based on a novel by H. G. [*sic*] McNeile. In: *Screen Romances,* Vol. 10, No. 61 (June, 1934), 52–53.
Brief, anonymous two-page fictionization with five photos from the 1934 United Artists film with Ronald Colman, Loretta Young, and Warner Oland.

"Bulldog Drummond's Bride." In: *Boy's Cinema & Modern Boy* (November 18, 1939), 14–18.
"Another grim adventure in which Bulldog Drummond finds himself up against an International crook of great cunning." Three photos from the Paramount film with John Howard as Drummond and Reginald Denny as Algy, with Heather Angel. Credits on page 18.

"Bulldog Drummond's Peril." In: *Boy's Cinema* (September 17, 1938), 13–16, 28.

"The fearless Englishman, up against a mysterious enemy, risks his life in a dangerous mission." Two photos from Paramount picture with John Howard, John Barrymore, Reginald Denny, E. E. Clive, and Halliwell Hobbes. Credits on page 24.

Burn, Witch, Burn! By A. Merritt. London: Methuen & Co., Ltd., Second Edition, 1935.
Dust jacket cover, with photo of Lionel Barrymore dressed as an old woman, from the MGM film, is pasted on the front flyleaf of this copy. Jacket has *Burn, Witch, Burn!* title and *The Devil Doll* with note *The Novel of the Film.* Title page and spine have *Burn* title.

"Busman's Honeymoon." Fictionized by Jean F. Webb. In: *Screen Romances*, Vol. 23, No. 137 (October 1940), 28–30, 52, 54, 56.
Five photos from the MGM film with Robert Montgomery as Lord Peter Wimsey, and Constance Cummings as Harriet Vane.

The Cabinet of Dr. Caligari. A film by Robert Wiene, Carl Mayer and Hans Janowitz; English translation and description of action by R. V. Adkinson. Paperback. New York: Simon and Schuster, c. 1972, c. 1919.
Description of each scene of the 1919 Decla-Bioscop/Goldwyn film, illustrated with photos from the movie.

"Calling Philo Vance." In: *Boy's Cinema*, No. 1064 (May 4, 1940), 7–14, 23–24.
"A tangled murder mystery, in which the death of a crooked designer of aeroplanes provides Philo Vance, the famous detective, with one of his biggest cases." Four photos from the 1940 Warner Bros. film with James Stephenson as Vance. Credits on page 24.

The "Canary" Murder Case. By S. S. Van Dine. New York: Grosset & Dunlap, c. 1927.
Four photos from the 1929 Paramount film with William Powell as Philo Vance. Dust jacket back cover has color artwork of Powell; front cover is a green index card with information on a murder.

"The Case of the Black Cat." In: *Boy's Cinema*, No. 910 (July 3, 1937), 1–12, 24–26.
"When a charred body is found in the bed of old Peter Laxter, an eccentric millionaire, after a fire, several different people are suspected of murder, and Perry Mason, lawyer-detective, sets out to solve the mystery. A black cat provides him with a clue, after an old caretaker is done to death,

but there is still another killing before the entirely unexpected truth is revealed. Starring Ricardo Cortez and June Travis." Cover and seven additional photos from the Warner Bros. film; credits listed on page 27.

"The Case of the Curious Bride." Fictionized by Mary Chadbourne-Brown. In: *Screen Romances*, Vol. 12, No. 73 (June 1935), 84–89.
Six photos from the 1935 Warner Bros. mystery with Warren William as Perry Mason. (The same issue has "The Mark of the Vampire.")

"The Case of the Howling Dog." Fictionized by Morton Savell. In: *Screen Romances*, Vol. 11, No. 66 (November 1934), 88–91, 109–110.
Seven photos from the Warner Bros. mystery with Warren William as Perry Mason, and Mary Astor.

The Cat and the Canary. By John Willard. London: The Readers Library Publishing Company Ltd., n.d. [No. 199].
Editor's Note refers to the 1927 film made by the "Universal Film Producing Company." No internal illustrations. Front cover of dust jacket has color drawing of black cat reaching out at canary, from behind grandfather clock showing midnight; skeletal ghostly figure glides in front. Back of dust jacket has drawing of a scene from the story, of monstrous hands reaching around to clutch figure in front of bookcase.

The Cat and the Canary. By Gerry Kingsley. Based on a screenplay by Radley Metzger. London: Sphere Books Limited, 1977. No. 0 7221 5266 3 Fiction/Film Tie-In.
Front cover has color photo of Carol Lynley in bed, being menaced by grotesque clutching hand; reflection of ugly villain's face appears in mirrored bed panel. (Different from the photo on the American paperback.) Credits from the Grenadier Films Ltd./Audubon Films Inc. Production are given on the back cover.

The Cat and the Canary. By Gerry Kingsley. Based on a screenplay by Radley Metzger. New York: Dale Books, 1978. No. 01219. "Novelization Copyright 1977 by Sphere Books, Lts. [*sic*] … Copyright 1978 by Dale Books, Inc."
Front and back cover have same color photo of Carol Lynley being menaced by clutching hand, from the 1978 Grenadier movie; this photo is different from that on the Sphere Books edition.

The Cat and the Canary: A Melodrama in Three Acts. By John Willard. New York: Samuel French, c. 1921. With the program of the first performance of the play as produced at the National Theatre, New York, February 7, 1922. Paperback.

Eight glossy photos from the stage play with Henry Hull and John Willard in the cast.

The Cat and the Canary: A Story of Love, Hate and Mystery. Based on the Motion Picture Story. By John Willard. New York: Jacobsen Publishing Company, Inc., c. 1927.

Title page notes "It's A UNIVERSAL JEWEL." This hardcover copy has a color photocopy of dust jacket, showing the same color artwork of Laura LaPlante that appears on cover of Jacobsen-Hodgkinson paperback (below). Photocopy of back of jacket, not on book, shows two b&w scenes from the 1927 silent film.

The Cat and the Canary: A Story of Love, Hate and Mystery. By John Willard. New York: Jacobsen-Hodgkinson Corporation, c. 1927. Paperback.

Cover has color artwork of Laura LaPlante. Back cover has two photos from the 1927 Universal movie; inside covers each have another. Eight additional photos printed within the text.

"The Cat Creeps." In: *Boy's Cinema*, No. 585 (February 28, 1931), 3–10, 26.

"One moment he was standing at her side—then came a padded footfall—a weird and eerie cry, and her companion vanished into space! A ghostly romance in a haunted house of a thousand horrors! Starring Helen Twelvetrees Raymond Hackett and Neil Hamilton." The cover of the magazine shows Twelvetrees and Hackett; there are seven internal photos and artwork of a creeping cat. An article about the set design of the film appears on page 2, along with the cast credits. This fictionization of the lost film presents the traditional plot, unlike the story "Horror By Night" in *Film Weekly* (April 25, 1931), which is simply "based on incidents in the Universal film, 'The Cat Creeps,'" and which gives a very different ending to the mystery.

The Cat Creeps (1931) see "Horror by Night"

"The Cat People." In: *Movie Story Magazine*, Vol. 14, No. 105 (January 1943), 44–45, 81–84.

Five photos from the 1942 Val Lewton RKO film with Simone Simon, Kent Smith, Jane Randolph, and Tom Conway. (The same issue has "I Married a Witch" and "One Dangerous Night.")

Chandu the Magician. Adapted from the photoplay "The Return of Chandu, the Magician" by Harry Earnshaw and Vera Oldham. Produced by Principal Pictures Corporation. Akron, Ohio, and New York: The Saalfield Publishing Company, c. 1935.

Children's book with color photo of Lugosi, in turban, on front cover and color photo of cat god Ubasti on back cover. Sixty-one internal b&w photos from the 1934 Principal/Victory serial in 12 chapters, *The Return of Chandu*. Advertisement at end of volume lists "Other Little Big Books" (not "Big Little").

"Charlie Chan at Monte Carlo." Fictionized by Henry LaCossit. In: *Screen Romances*, Vol. 17, No. 104 (January 1938), 60-63, 104–106.

Six photos, over background of seventh photo of roulette table, from the 20th Century–Fox film with Warner Oland, Keye Luke, and Harold Huber.

Charlie Chan Carries On. By Earl Derr Biggers. New York: Grosset & Dunlap, c. 1930.

Four photos from the lost 1931 Fox movie in which Warner Oland first appeared as Chan. (*The Black Camel* is the first surviving film with Oland as Chan.)

"Charlie Chan's Courage." In: *The Film Star Weekly*, Vol. 5, No. 105 (December 22, 1934), 27.

Not a fictionization, but a one-page plot summary of the 1934 Fox film with Warner Oland, with three photos. Based on the novel *The Chinese Parrot*; this is considered a lost film.

"Charlie Chan's Greatest Case." In: *The Film Star Weekly*, Vol. 3, No. 64 (February 10, 1934), 20-21.

One photo from the lost 1934 Fox film with Warner Oland as Chan. An additional photo of Oland as Chan appears on page 2.

"Charlie McCarthy, Detective." Fictionized by Gordon Field. In: *Screen Romances*, Vol. 18, No. 130 (March 1940), 37, 76–80.

Two photos from the 1940 Universal film with Edgar Bergen and Charlie McCarthy, Robert Cummings, Constance Moore, Edgar Kennedy, Harold Huber, Warren Hymer, and Milburn Stone.

The Chinese Parrot. By Earl Derr Biggers. London: The Readers Library Publishing Company Ltd., n.d. [Unnumbered; apparently different from No. 210 in Richard Williams's *Readers Library* bibliography: No. 210 listed as having 256 pages; this copy has 252 pp. plus one unnumbered ad page at end.]

Editor's Note refers to "Universal Jewel" picture produced by Paul Leni, starring Marion Nixon and Hobart Bosworth, and "which is now to be released in Great Britain." No internal photos. Color dust jacket shows artwork only, no photos; "Universal Picture" appears in small type on front cover. *The Chinese Parrot*, from 1928, was the second Charlie Chan film, after Pathé's 1926 ten-chapter serial *The House Without a Key* (now a lost film), with George Kuwa as Chan. *The Chinese Parrot* (1928), also now lost, featured Kamiyama Sojin as Chan; it was Paul Leni's follow-up film to *The Cat and The Canary*.

The Chink in the Armour see *The House of Peril*

Circus Queen Murder see *About the Murder of the Circus Queen*

"The Circus Shadow." In: *Boy's Cinema*, No. 968 (July 2, 1938), Cover and
    2–12, 26, 28.
    "The day after Senor Martinet, a star equestrian, has announced his intention of taking over Gillespie's Mammoth Circus he is killed during a performance, and that night a cloaked and hooded figure appears and another murder is committed. Jim Quinn, the circus press agent, sets a trap and is himself attacked—with startling consequences. A tense and eerie drama, starring Charles Quigley, with Rita Hayworth and Marc Lawrence." Six photos from the Columbia Pictures film.

Clash of the Titans. A novel by Alan Dean Foster. Based on the original
    screenplay by Beverly Cross. New York: Warner Books, 1981. No. 93–675.
    Four double-sided pages with fourteen b&w photos from the Ray Harryhausen MGM movie; front cover is color artwork.

Clash of the Titans. Golden comic No. 11290-20. New York: Golden Press,
    1981.
    Magazine-size comic book version, with color cardboard covers, of the 1981 MGM movie. Front cover has color artwork and eight color photos; inside front cover has ten b&w photos of human characters with actors' names given, and extra photo of mechanical owl Bubo. Additional film credits are given on title page. Inside back cover has seven additional photos and two artwork representations of monsters from the movie.

Cleek of Scotland Yard. By T. W. Hanshew. (Note: T. W. here) New York:
    A. L. Burt Company, c. 1912, 1914.
    Thirteen photos on eight pages from the movie; also dye-ink drawing on front cover. Title page has subtitle note, "Being the record of the further life and adventures of that remarkable detective genius, 'The Man of

the Forty Faces,' once known to the police as 'The Vanishing Cracksman'."
Same page has the note "Illustrated with Photographs of the Motion Pictures By Courtesy of Thomas A. Edison, Inc."

Cleek of Scotland Yard. By T. P. Hanshew. (Note: T. P. here) Garden City,
  N.Y.: Doubleday, Page & Company, 1922.
  One photo (frontispiece) from the movie; same photo as in the above
copy. Title page says, "Frontispiece from photographs of the motion pictures by courtesy of Thomas A. Edison, Inc."

The Climax. Novelized by Florence Jay Lewis. New York: Books, Inc., 1944.
  Cover color photo on dust jacket shows Boris Karloff and Susanna Foster from the 1944 Universal film; Karloff's face and hand are tinted green.
No internal photos. (Semi-sequel to Universal's *Phantom of the Opera*, using
some of the same sets.)

"The Climax." Fictionized by Helen McCloy. In: *Screen Romances*, Vol. 28,
  No. 184 (September 1944), 44–46, 74, 76, 78–79.
  Seven photos from the Universal Pictures film with Boris Karloff,
Susanna Foster, Turhan Bey, and Gale Sondergaard.

A Coffin for Demetrios. By Eric Ambler. Cleveland and New York: The
  World Publishing Company, 1944.
  Dust jacket has seven green-tinted photos from the 1944 Warner Bros.
film with Sydney Greenstreet and Peter Lorre, entitled *Mask of Demetrios.*

Comedy of Terrors. A Novel by Elsie Lee. Based on Richard Matheson's
  Screenplay. New York: Lancer Books, 1964. No. 70-067.
  Front and back covers have seven photos from the 1964 American-Inter-
national picture.

The Conspirators. By Frederick Prokosch. New York: Grosset & Dunlap,
  1943.
  Dust jacket has seven photos from the 1944 Warner Bros. picture with
Paul Henried, Sydney Greenstreet, and Peter Lorre.

Corruption. By Peter Saxon. London: Sphere Books Limited, 1969. No.
  24562.
  Front and back covers have color photos from the Columbia Pictures film
with Peter Cushing; Cushing appears in the front photo, holding a bloody
knife.

Countess Dracula. By Michael Parry. London: Sphere Books Limited, 1971.
   Front and back covers have photos of Ingrid Pitt from the Hammer Production. (Title page of this copy is autographed by Ingrid Pitt.)

Craig Kennedy Stories see *The Romance of Elaine*

Creature from the Black Lagoon. By Carl Dreadstone. Adapted from the screenplay by Arthur Ross and Harry Essex, from a story by Maurice Zimm. With an introduction by Ramsey Campbell. New York: Berkley Publishing Corporation, 1977.
   Numerous photos from the 1954 Universal film.

"The Crosby Case." Fictionized by Miriam Rogers. In: *Screen Romances*, Vol. 10, No. 60 (May 1934), 87–90, 92, 104.
   Five photos from the 1934 Universal mystery with Onslow Stevens, Warren Hymer, and Edward Van Sloan.

Curse of Frankenstein/Horror of Dracula. Story Adaptation by Russ Jones and Joe Orlando, Lettering by Ben Oda. New York: Warren Publishing Company, 1964. Famous Films No. 2.
   Photo-story magazine of the two Hammer films with Peter Cushing and Christopher Lee.

"Curse of the Cat People." In: *Movie Story Magazine*, Vol. 16, No. 118 (February 1944), 44–45, 99–102, 106, 108, 110.
   One double-page spread photo on pages 44–45, of Simone Simon and young Ann Carter, from 1944 Val Lewton RKO film. Credits on page 45. (The same issue has "The Lodger.")

Day of the Arrow see *13*

Deadline at Dawn. By William Irish. Cleveland and New York: The World Publishing Company, 1946.
   Title on two-page photo background; two double-sided photo pages bound in; endpapers illustrated with photos from the 1946 RKO Radio film with Susan Hayward. Dust jacket has six additional photos.

Death in the Doll's House. By Hannah Lees and Lawrence Bachman. Movie title *Shadow on the Wall.* New York: Dell Publishing Company, Inc., c. 1943. No. 356.
   Map-back paperback with color photo on front of Ann Sothern and Zachary Scott from the MGM film.

"The Death Kiss." In: *The Film Star Weekly*, Vol. 2, No. 31 (June 24, 1933), 5–7.

"Just a film tragedy scene—but it turned into a mysterious tragedy of real life." Two photos from the 1933 Ideal Pictures/K. B. S. Productions film with David Manners, Bela Lugosi, and Edward Van Sloan. All three appear in the photos.

The Deerslayer. By James Fenimore Cooper. New York: Grosset & Dunlap, n.d.

Included here for its Bela Lugosi tie-in. Four photos from The Mingo Pictures Company silent film; Lugosi appears a Chingachgook on frontispiece and on plate facing page 414. The Mingo version was a 1923 American release of part of the 1920 German film *Lederstrumpf* (Leatherstocking) directed by Arthur Wellin, filmed in the forests of the Rhine Valley. This edition includes a dedication page to The Boy Scouts of America.

Detective Dick Tracy and the Spider Gang. Racine, Wisconsin: Whitman Publishing Company, c. 1937. Big Little Book.

Title page reads: "*from the* MOVIE SERIAL / *Based on the Famous Comic Strip Character / By* CHESTER GOULD / *Retold from the* Republic Motion Picture / *with* Ralph Byrd *as* Dick Tracy / Kay Hughes *as* Gwen / Smiley Burnette *as* Mike McGurk / Lee Van Atta *as* Junior." Eighty-one internal b&w photos plus colored photo on back cover; front cover shows Gould drawing of Tracy in profile; spine shows drawing of spider with red eyes. Front cover reads: "Story of the Motion Picture/Republic Serial."

The Devil Doll see *Burn, Witch, Burn!*

"Devil Girl From Mars." In: *Picture Show & Film Pictorial*, Vol. 62, No. 1630 (June 26, 1954), 5–6, 12.

Four photos from the British Lion film with Hugh McDermott, Hazel Court, and Patricia Laffan. Credits on page 10.

Devilday see *Madhouse*

"Devil's Island." Fictionized by Robert Arthur. In: *Screen Romances*, 18, 115 (December 1938), 48–49, 114–16.

One photo of Boris Karloff from the Warner Bros. film; credits on page 49. (The same issue has "The Lady Vanishes.)

Die, Monster, Die! Dell comic No. 12–175–603. New York: Dell Publishing Co., Inc., 1965.

Comic book version of the 1965 American-International film. Front cover has two color photos, one of Boris Karloff, one of Nick Adams and Susan Farmer. Inside front cover has four b&w photos and film credits.

Dinosaurus! Dell Movie Classic comic No. 1120. New York: Dell Publishing Co., Inc., 1960.
Comic book version of the 1960 Universal International film. Front cover has color artwork; inside front cover has five b&w photos and screen credits.

Dr. Cyclops. By Will Garth. New York: Phoenix Press, 1940.
Dust jacket (only) has green-tinted artwork depiction of Albert Dekker as Dr. Cyclops, in upper left corner, glaring down at small, running female figure; spine shows same image of Dekker, reduced; tie-in to the Paramount film.

"Dr. Cyclops." In: *Movie Story Magazine*, 14, 73 (May 1940), 36–38, 85–90.
Ten photos from the 1940 Paramount film with Albert Dekker. Additional photo of Dekker appears in table of contents, page 4; full page ad on page 7 shows numerous small artwork scenes from the film. (Different from Kuttner novelization, below.)

"Dr. Cyclops." By Henry Kuttner. In: *Thrilling Wonder Stories*, 16, 3 (June 1940), 14–32.
Two photos from the 1940 Paramount film; also colored drawing on magazine cover.

Dr. Jekyll and Mr. Hyde. By Robert Louis Stevenson. New York: Grosset & Dunlap, n.d.
Seven photos from the 1931 Paramount film with Fredric March; one of the photos is a double-page spread. Dust jacket has color photo/artwork of March, with artwork of John Barrymore–looking Hyde over his shoulder. (The dust jacket is similar to the earlier Barrymore poster and subsequent Spencer Tracy jacket illustration.)

Dr. Jekyll and Mr. Hyde. By Robert Louis Stevenson. New York: Grosset & Dunlap, n.d.
Color dust jacket has yellowish-green tinted photo of Spencer Tracy from the 1941 MGM version, with an artwork Hyde likeness resembling the John Barrymore makeup. (Dust jacket similar to earlier Fredric March jacket illustration, and Barrymore poster.)

Dr. Jekyll and Mr. Hyde. Original story by Robert Louis Stevenson. Adapted by Horace J. Elias from the MGM movie starring Spencer Tracy. New York: Harper & Row, 1976. No. P/BN 5053.

Verso pages contain text, recto pages show photos from the Spencer Tracy version. Cover has photo of Tracy as Hyde from the 1941 MGM film.

Dr. Jekyll and Mr. Hyde See also *Merry Men, Modern Mystery and Adventure Novels,* and *The Strange Case of Dr. Jekyll and Mr. Hyde.*

"Dr. Jekyll and Mr. Hyde." In: *Boy's Cinema,* No. 138 (September 24, 1932), 17–20, 27.
"The grim story of a doctor who changed into another being, and how the evil side triumphed. Starring Fredric March." Four photos from the Paramount film; cast list on page 2.

"Dr. Jekyll and Mr. Hyde." In: *Movie Story Magazine,* Vol. 16, No. 87 (July 1941), 22–25, 65–70.
Four photos from the 1941 MGM film with Spencer Tracy, Ingrid Bergman, and Lana Turner. Film credits given on page 23.

"Dr. Jekyll and Mr. Hyde." Fictionized by Virginia Vale. In: *Screen Romances,* Vol. 25, No. 147 (August 1941), 26, 65–66.
"A Short-Short Adaptation," with three photos, of the 1941 MGM film with Spencer Tracy, Ingrid Bergman, and Lana Turner.

Dr. Jekyll and Mr. Hyde and Other Stories. By Robert Louis Stevenson. New York: Pocket Books, Inc., second printing, October 1941. No. 123.
Paperback. Cover has photo of Spencer Tracy as Dr. Jekyll, drawing of Mr. Hyde, from the 1941 MGM movie.

Dr. Phibes. By William Goldstein. Based on the screenplay by James Whiton and William Goldstein. New York: Award Books; London: Tandem Books, 1971. No. A869S.
Front cover has b&w photo of Vincent Price and Virginia North (as Vulnavia) from the American-International film *The Abominable Dr. Phibes.*

Dr. Phibes Rises Again. By William Goldstein. New York: Award Books, 1972. No. AN1069.
Color photo cover shows skeletal hands grasping blonde woman (not from film). Back cover gives credits list for the American-International Picture starring Vincent Price, Robert Quarry, and Peter Cushing.

Dracula. By Bram Stoker. New York: Grosset & Dunlap, c. 1897.
Four photos from the 1931 Universal film with Bela Lugosi. The dust

jacket has a color drawing on the front, and a blue-tinted picture of Lugosi standing on Dracula's castle steps, on the back.

Dracula. By Bram Stoker. New York: Permabooks, Second Printing, May, 1958. No. M 4088. Spine has additional "8" below M / 4088.
Cover: "The most famous horror story ever told—now a great motion picture released through Universal-International." One photo of Christopher Lee from the Hammer film *Horror of Dracula.*

Dracula. By Bram Stoker. New York: A Jove Book, 1979. No. K5347.
Twenty-four glossy pages bound in with synopsis, color photos, and credits from the Universal picture with Frank Langella and Laurence Olivier. Front and back cover have wrap-around color photo of Langella and actress from the movie.

Dracula: The Ultimate Illustrated Edition of the World-Famous Vampire Play. Hamilton Deane & John L. Balderston. Edited and annotated by David J. Skal. New York: St. Martin's Press, 1993.
Contains texts of the 1924 and 1927 versions of the play with numerous photo and drawing illustrations.

Dracula: The Vampire Play in Three Acts. Dramatized by Hamilton Deane and John L. Balderston. New York, London: Samuel French. Copyright 1927 by John L. Balderston; copyright 1933 by Samuel French.
Text of play illustrated with three glossy photos from the 1927 Broadway production with Bela Lugosi and Edward Van Sloan, with Bernard Jukes as Renfield. Includes extensive Electrical Plot, Property Plot, Notes on Production, Publicity Notes, and stage diagrams.

Dracula's Daughter. By Carl Dreadstone. Adapted from the story by John L. Balderston. With and introduction by Ramsey Campbell. New York: Berkley Publishing Corporation, 1977.
Numerous photos from the 1936 Universal film.

"The Dragon Murder Case." Fictionized by Nan Bouve. In: *Screen Romances*, Vol. 11, No. 65 (October 1934), 72–75, 100–101.
Four photos from the First National picture with Warren William as Philo Vance, with Lyle Talbot, Eugene Pallette, and George E. Stone.

"The Dragon Murder Case." In: *Film Star Weekly*, Vol. 5, No. 114, (January 26, 1935), 9–11.
Two photos from the Warner Bros. film with Warren William as Philo Vance.

The Dragon Murder Case see *Philo Vance Murder Cases*

"Dressed to Kill." In: *Movie Story Magazine*, Vol. 21, No. 146 (June 1946), 50, 70–71.
Two photos from the Universal Picture with Basil Rathbone as Sherlock Holmes and Nigel Bruce as Watson, with Patricia Morison. (The same issue has "The Blue Dahlia.")

Edgar Allan Poe's Tales of Terror. Dell Movie Classic comic No. 12–793–302. New York: Dell Publishing Co. Inc., 1962.
Comic book version of the 1962 American-International Picture with Vincent Price, Peter Lorre, Basil Rathbone, and Debra Paget. Front cover has three color photos from the film; inside front cover has five b&w photos and credits.

"Ellery Queen's Penthouse Mystery." Fictionized by Helen McCloy. In: *Screen Romances*, Vol. 24, No. 144 (May 1941), 36, 60–65.
"Nikki had a nose for mysteries—and a heart that belonged exclusively to the famous Ellery Queen." One sepia photo from the Columbia Film with Ralph Bellamy, Margaret Lindsay, Charlie Grapewin, Anna May Wong, and Mantan Moreland.

End of the World. By Dean Owen. New York: Ace Books, Inc., 1962. No. D-548.
Two photos on front cover, two on back, from the American-International Picture with Ray Milland, Jean Hagen, and Frankie Avalon.

The Exorcist. By William Peter Blatty. New York et al.: Harper & Row, Publishers, c. 1971, 1973.
Eight page section with sixteen photos from the 1973 Warner Bros. movie; dust jacket has a photo of Blatty. Special band over dust jacket advertises "A Special Motion Picture Edition."

Exploits of Elaine: A Detective Novel. By Arthur B. Reeve. New York: Hearst's International Library Co., 1915.
Twenty illustrations from the 1914 Pathé Players serial with Pearl White; dust jacket has color tinted photo/drawing of detective Craig Kennedy and Elaine warding off the Clutching Hand leading a group of villains.

Eyes in the Night, Photoplay Title of The Odor of Violets. By Baynard Kendrick. New York: Grosset & Dunlap, c. 1940, 1941.
Dust jacket (only) has one cover photo from the 1942 MGM movie with Edward Arnold and Ann Harding.

"A Face in the Fog." In: *Boy's Cinema*, No. 864 (July 4, 1936), 13–20.

"Who is the Fiend? A strange, hunch-backed figure that flits through the darkness of the night and strikes, leaving no clue. A thriller with a strange climax, starring Lloyd Hughes and June Collyer." Four photos from the Victory Pictures film, set in an old theater; somewhat like Universal's 1928 *The Last Warning.* Credits on page 27. (The same issue has *Flash Gordon*, Episode 9, "Fighting the Dragon.")

"The Falcon in Mexico." In: *Movie Story Magazine*, Vol. 17, No. 124 (August 1944), 51, 96–104, 106.

Two photos (pages 51 and 101) from the 1944 RKO Radio picture with Tom Conway. (The same issue has "The Mummy's Ghost.")

"The Falcon's Alibi." In: *Movie Story Magazine*, Vol. 20, No. 141 (January 1946), 56, 97–101.

One photo from the 1945 RKO Radio Picture with Tom Conway and Elisha Cook, Jr. (The same issue has "The House of Dracula" and "The Spider.")

The Fall of the House of Usher. By Edgar Allan Poe. London: Digit Books; Brown, Watson Limited, n.d. No. R461.

Cover has color artwork of woman in glass coffin, tied-in to the Anglo-American Film starring Vincent Price.

The Fall of the House of Usher see *Tales of Mystery and Imagination*

Fallen Angel. By Marty Holland. Chicago: Century Publications, c. 1945. Paperback.

"Condensed" story with color drawing on cover of Alice Faye, Dana Andrews, and others from the 1946 Otto Preminger film from 20th Century–Fox.

Fantastic Tales. By Edgar Allan Poe. London: New English Library, 1969. No. NEL 2570.

The front cover says "Now a series of spellbinding films." A color photo of Jane Fonda is on the front; the back cover has color photos of Fonda and Brigitte Bardot from the Les Films Marceau production *Spirits of the Dead* (1969), listed here under its French title *Histoires Extraordinaires.* The back cover also has two b&w photos, of Christopher Lee and of Vincent Price bending over a prostrate Lee, from American-International's *The Oblong Box* (1969).

Fantastic Voyage. Isaac Asimov, based on a screenplay by Harry Kleiner. New York: Bantam Books, October 1966. No. H3177.
Front cover has a b&w photo montage; back cover has a color photo from the 20th Century–Fox movie.

Fantastic Voyage. Gold Key Comic. Poughkeepsie, New York: K.K. Publications, Inc., 1966. No. 10178–702.
Front cover has four color photos and artwork from the 20th Century–Fox film; the back cover has two. The inside front cover has three b&w photos and movie credits; inside back cover has four b&w photos.

"Fantastic Voyage." Adapted by Jean Francis Webb. In: *Screen Stories*, Vol. 65, No. 4 (April 1966), 41–45, 70–73.
Eight photos from the 20th Century–Fox film with Stephen Boyd and Raquel Welch. (The same issue has "The Ghost and Mr. Chicken.")

Farewell, My Lovely. By Raymond Chandler. Cleveland and New York: The World Publishing Company, 1944.
Dust jacket has seven photos from the 1944 RKO movie *Murder, My Sweet,* with Dick Powell.

"Farewell, My Lovely." In: *Movie Story Magazine,* Vol. 18, No. 127 (November 1944), 44–47, 91–94.
Five photos from the RKO film with Dick Powell, Claire Trevor, and Mike Mazurki.

The Film Star Weekly— "Charlie Chan's Courage," "Charlie Chan's Greatest Case," "The Death Kiss," "The Dragon Murder Case," "The King Murder," "The Mask of Fu Manchu," "The Mummy," "The Night Club Lady," "The Penguin Pool Mystery," "Secrets of Wu Sin," and "The 13th Guest."

Film Weekly—"Horror by Night" (*The Cat Creeps*).

First Men In The Moon. By H. G. Wells. New York: Ballantine Books, third printing, December 1964 [first printing January 1963]. No. U2232.
Front cover is a color artwork depiction of iron moon craft from the 1963 Columbia Pictures film with Edward Judd, Martha Hyer, and Lionel Jeffries, directed by Nathan Juran. Special effects by Ray Harryhausen.

First Men in the Moon. Gold Key comic No. 10132–503. New York: Dell Publishing Co., Inc., 1964.

Front cover has three color photos from the Columbia Pictures movie; inside front cover has five b&w photos and film credits. Back cover is green-tinted artwork montage of scenes from the film. Special effects by Ray Harryhausen.

"The First Men in the Moon." Adapted by George Scullin. In: *Screen Stories*, Vol. 63, No. 12 (December 1964), 14–16, 80–84.
Four photos from the 1964 Columbia Pictures film with Edward Judd, Martha Hyer, and Lionel Jeffries. Special effects by Ray Harryhausen.

"Flash Gordon." In: *Boy's Cinema*, No. 860 (June 6, 1936), 21–24, 27; No. 861 (June 13, 1936), 21–24, 28; No. 864 (July 4, 1936), 21–24, 27; No. 868 (August 1, 1936), 19–22, 28.
"Beyond the stratosphere to a new world where science marches hand in hand with savagery. Follow the adventures of a young American on the strange planet of Mongo, realm of monsters and domain of the War-Lord Ming. An unforgettable serial of thrills and suspense, starring Buster Crabbe and Jean Rogers." No. 860: Episode 5, "The Destroying Ray"; No. 861: Episode 6, "Flaming Torture"; No. 864, Episode 9, "Fighting the Fire Dragon"; No. 868, "Rocketing to Earth"; from the Universal production, also starring Charles Middleton. Five b&w photos in each issue. (No. 860 also has "The Lone Wolf Returns"; No. 864, "A Face in the Fog"; No. 868, "The Rogue's Tavern.")

The Flesh and the Fiends. By Allan Norwood. London: Corgi Books; Transworld Publishers, 1960. No. SN786.
Color artwork front cover; back cover has b&w photo from Triad Production film with Peter Cushing. This story of body-snatchers Burke and Hare was also released under various other titles: *Mania, The Fiendish Ghouls, Psycho-Killers.*

Forbidden Planet. By W. J. Stuart. New York: Bantam Books, 1956. No. A1433.
Front cover shows color artwork from the MGM film; back cover has one b&w photo.

"Forbidden Planet." Adapted by Will. F. Jenkins. In: *Screen Stories*, Vol. 55, No. 4 (April 1956), 39–41, 60–63.
Five photos from the MGM film with Walter Pidgeon, Anne Francis, and Leslie Nielsen. Additional full-page ad with artwork appears on page 3.

Frankenstein. By Mary W. Shelley. New York: Grosset & Dunlap, n.d.

Seven blue-tinted photos from the 1931 Universal film with Boris Karloff; one of the photos is a double-page spread. The dust jacket has a green-tinted photo/drawing of the monster's face against a red background, lurking above a photo/drawing of Mae Clarke, with red hair and in a light green dress, on a bed, corresponding to the photo opposite page 122.

Frankenstein. By Mary W. Shelley. London: The Readers Library Publishing Company Ltd., n.d. No. 364.

One b&w photo (retouched) from the 1931 film showing Karloff in supplication posture, on front panel of dust jacket; no internal photos. Dust jacket has title *Frankenstein: The Man Who Made A Monster.* Above the jacket title: "A Universal Film/I live!/I breathe!/I walk!/I see!/What am I?/Man or/Monster?" Title page reads *Frankenstein, or The Modern Prometheus*; t.p. note adds, "On this famous story Universal have [*sic*] based a film starring Colin Clive, Boris Karloff, Frederick Kerr and Mae Clarke."

"Frankenstein Meets the Wolf Man." In: *Movie Story Magazine*, Vol. 14, No. 107 (March 1943), 40–41, 73–74, 76–78.

Five photos from the 1943 Universal film, showing Lon Chaney, Bela Lugosi, Ilona Massey, Patric Knowles, and Maria Ouspenskaya. (A fictionization of "Casablanca" appears in the same issue.)

The G-String Murders. By Gypsy Rose Lee. Cleveland and New York: The World Publishing Company, 1944; Tower Books Edition. seventh printing, February 1944.

Dust jacket has six photos from the 1943 United Artists movie *Lady of Burlesque* with Barbara Stanwyck. Jacket also has a subtitle, *The Story of a Burlesque Girl*, not on the title page.

The G-String Murders see *Lady of Burlesque*

"Gaslight." In: *Movie Story Magazine*, Vol. 17, No. 12 (July 1944), 28–31, 87–96.

Five photos, plus full-color cover, from the 1944 MGM film with Charles Boyer, Ingrid Bergman, Joseph Cotten, and Angela Lansbury. (The same issue has "The Ghost Catchers.")

"The Gay Falcon." In: *Movie Story Magazine*, Vol. 16, No. 89 (September 1941), 42, 86–91.

One photo from the RKO-Radio Picture with George Sanders as the Falcon.

"The Ghost and Mr. Chicken." Adapted by Chris Kane. In: *Screen Stories*,
Vol. 65, No. 4 (April 1966), 46–49, 67–69.
Eight photos from the Universal film with Don Knotts. (The same issue
has "Fantastic Voyage.")

The Ghost Breaker. By Charles W. Goddard and Paul Dickey. New York:
Hearst's International Library Company, 1915.
Title page says "A Novel Based Upon the Play." Twelve b&w photos
from the 1913 stage play production with H. B. Warner as Warren Jarvis,
Katherine Emmet as the Spanish princess, and William Sampson as the
negro servant. (*New York Times* theatrical review dates play in 1913; *Horror in Silent Films* says 1909. The difference indicates performance vs. publication dates.) Warner also starred in the 1914 film version. This is the story
that eventually formed the basis of the 1940 Paramount film, *The Ghost
Breakers* (plural), with Bob Hope and Paulette Goddard.

The Ghost Breaker. By Charles W. Goddard & Paul Dickey. New York: Star
Library Company, c. 1915. Star Fiction Library No. 8. Paperback.
Twelve b&w photos from the 1913 stage play production with H. B.
Warner as Warren Jarvis, Katherine Emmet as the Spanish princess, and
William Sampson as the negro servant. Warner also starred in the 1914
film version. Front cover has color drawing of Warren Jarvis and Maria
Theresa characters. Back cover has blue and white illustration of the dust
jacket cover of the Hearst's International Library Co.'s hardcover photoplay edition of *The Exploits of Elaine.* Inside front cover of *The Ghost Breaker*
says *Exploits* novel also available as Star Fiction Library No. 16 (paperback
with "Twenty illustrations from the photo-play").

The Ghost Breaker: A Melodramatic Farce in Four Acts. By Paul Dickey and
Charles Goddard. New York and London: Samuel French, c. 1909; Copyright assigned, 1914, to Sanger & Jordan.
Play script illustrated with four photos from the stage production with
H. B. Warner. The same four photos appear in novelized version, above.

"The Ghost Breakers." Fiction Version by Norman Russell. In: *Movie Mirror*, Vol. 17, No. 3 (August 1940), 30, 70–73.
Four photos from the 1940 Paramount film with Bob Hope, Paulette
Goddard, and Willie Best.

"The Ghost Breakers." By Bob Hope. In: *Movie Story Magazine*, Vol. 14,
No. 76 (August 1940), 26–27, 66–68.
Not a novelization of the Paramount film story but "An On-the-Set Pre-

view of *The Ghost Breakers* By Bob Hope." Hope—if he is indeed the author—breezily accounts behind-the-scenes stories of the filming. Six photos appear with the story on pages 26–27; additional photos from the film appear on pages 4 and 15; page 7 is a full-page ad for the film. The magazine cover is a color photo of Hope and Paulette Goddard.

"The Ghost Catchers." In: *Movie Story Magazine*, Vol. 17, No. 12 (July 1944), 46–47, 97–102.
   Three photos from the 1944 Universal Picture with Ole Olsen and Chick Johnson, Martha O'Driscoll, Lon Chaney, Jr., Leo Carillo, and Andy Devine. (The same issue has "Gaslight.")

"The Ghost of Frankenstein." In: *Movie Story Magazine*, Vol. 18, No. 96 (April 1942), 34–35, 86–92.
   Three photos from the Universal film with Lon Chaney, Jr., Evelyn Ankers, Sir Cedric Hardwicke, Lionel Atwill, Bela Lugosi, and Ralph Bellamy. An additional photo is of Boris Karloff as the Monster (not inappropriately—clips from the original *Frankenstein* do appear in *Ghost*).

"The Ghost Steps Out." In: *Movie Story Magazine*, Vol. 21, No. 147 (July 1946), 40–43, 91–93.
   Three photos from the Universal film released under the title *The Time of Their Lives* (August 16, 1946) with Abbott and Costello, and Marjorie Reynolds.

The Ghost Train. By Ruth Alexander and Arnold Ridley. Adapted from the play by Arnold Ridley. London: The Readers Library Publishing Company Ltd., 1927 [No. 126].
   Dust jacket has color artwork on front and back. Front panel shows ghostly greenish switchman, with staring eyes, at side of green locomotive. Back cover shows four people in waiting room staring apprehensively through broken window (apparently a scene from the 1927 Gainsborough Productions film version).

The Ghouls. Edited by Peter Haining. Introduction by Vincent Price. Afterword by Christopher Lee. New York: Stein and Day, 1971.
   Anthology of eighteen short stories from which horror films were made, illustrated with photos from the respective movies: *The Devil in a Convent* by Francis Oscar Mann; *The Lunatics* by Edgar Allan Poe; *Puritan Passions* by Nathaniel Hawthorne; *Phantom of the Opera* by Gaston Leroux; *The Magician* by Somerset Maugham; *Freaks* by Tod Robbins; *Most Dangerous Game* by Richard Connell; *Dracula's Daughter* by Bram Stoker; *All That*

Money Can Buy by Stephen Vincent Benét; *The Body Snatcher* by Robert Louis Stevenson; *The Beast With Five Fingers* by W. F. Harvey; *The Beast From 20,000 Fathoms* by Ray Bradbury; *The Fly* by George Langelaan; *Black Sunday* by Nikolai Gogol; *Incident at Owl Creek* by Ambrose Bierce; *Monster of Terror* by H. P. Lovecraft; *The Skull* by Robert Bloch; and *The Oblong Box* by Edgar Allan Poe.

The Girl in the Moon. By Thea von Harbou. Translated by Baroness Von Hutten. London: The Readers Library Publishing Company Ltd., n.d. No. 304.
   Title page notes: "Illustrated with scenes from the photo-play / A Gaumont-Ufa Film / Starring Gerda Maurus and Willy Fritsch." With eight brown and white photos on four double-sided plates from the 1929 Fritz Lang film. (This copy lacks dust jacket.)

The Glass Key. By Dashiell Hammett. New York: Grosset & Dunlap, c. 1931.
   Dust jacket has one photo from the 1942 Paramount movie with Alan Ladd and Veronica Lake.

The Golden Voyage of Sinbad. A novel by Steve Hart. From the screenplay by Brian Clemens based on a story by Brian Clemens and Ray Harryhausen. New York: Warner Paperback Library, 1974. No. 75–625.
   Eight double-sided pages with thirty-eight b&w photos from the Columbia Pictures movie; front cover has color artwork.

The Golden Voyage of Sinbad. New York: Marvel Comics Group, 1974. Marvel Comic 8 Aug 02186.
   Comic book version of the second half of *Golden Voyage* story, "Based on the thrilling Motion Picture … A Charles Schneer Production Presented by Columbia Pictures" on cover; "Freely adapted from the screenplay by Brian Clemens" on first page. No photos or artwork from the film; first half of story recapitulated on page 2.

Gorgo. By Carson Bingham. Based on an original story by Eugene Lourie, screenplay by John Loring and David Hyatt. Derby, Connecticut: Monarch Books, 1960. No. MM603.
   Front cover has orangish tinted photo of monster from the King Brothers movie; back cover similarly tinted photo composite from movie.

"The Gorilla." By Virginia Brunswick Smith. In: *Moving Picture Stories*, Vol. 30, No. 780 (December 6, 1927), 13–16.

Three photos from the lost 1927 First National film with Charlie Murray, Fred Kelsey, Tully Marshall, Alice Day, and Walter Pidgeon.

"The Gorilla." In: *Movie Story Magazine*, Vol. 13, No. 62 (June 1939), 35–37, 68–71.
Page 35 is a montage showing numerous stars of the 20th Century–Fox film; six more photos appear on pages 36–37, including the Ritz Brothers, Lionel Atwill, and Bela Lugosi. An additional photo appears in the table of contents, page 4.

The Gracie Allen Murder Case. By S. S. Van Dine. New York: Charles Scribner's Sons, 1938.
This Scribner's copy has the dust jacket from the Grosset & Dunlap reprint, with one photo on the back showing Gracie Allen and Warren William, as Philo Vance, from the Paramount film.

"The Gracie Allen Murder Case." In: *Movie Story Magazine*, Vol. 13, No. 63 (July 1939), 43–45, 64–69.
Six photos from the 1939 Paramount picture with Gracie Allen as herself and Warren William as Philo Vance. Additional photo appears in table of contents, page 4.

"The Gracie Allen Murder Case." In: *Boy's Cinema & Modern Boy*, No. 1045 (December 23, 1939), 13–16.
"A flower, a cigarette, a perfume bottle—these are the clues to a murder mystery which the hilarious Gracie Allen wise-cracks wide open! A story adapted from the Paramount picture that is one big laugh from start to finish." Two photos from 1939 film with Warren William as Philo Vance. Credits on page 16.

Grass. By Merian C. Cooper. New York & London: G. P Putnam's Sons, The Knickerbocker Press, 1925.
Tie-in volume to the Famous Players–Lasky documentary, distributed by Paramount Pictures. Title page adds, "With Sixty-Four Illustrations From Photographs By Ernest Beaumont Schoedsack." Cooper and Schoedsack went on to produce *King Kong* seven years later. Fly leaf autographed by Cooper: "For W. C. Robertson, who I respect as a man and an editor—with best wishes—Merian C. Cooper."

The Green Goddess. By Louise Jordan Miln. New York: A. L. Burt Company, c. 1922.
Four photos from the 1923 Goldwyn film with George Arliss.

The Greene Murder Case. By S. S. Van Dine. New York: Grosset & Dunlap, c. 1927, 1928.
   Eight photos from the 1929 Paramount film with William Powell as
Philo Vance. Dust jacket has "typed" police report form on front cover; back
cover is color artwork of Powell/Vance.

Gulliver's Travels. By Jonathan Swift. With an Introduction by Maxwell
   Geismar. New York: Washington Square Press, Inc., Third Printing, Feb-
   ruary 1961. No. W251.
   Front cover shows color artwork rendering—not from movie—of Lil-
liputians binding a standing Gulliver's legs. Between his legs is the copy,
"This world-famous adventure classic has now been made into a breath-
taking movie, THE THREE WORLDS OF GULLIVER Produced by Charles H.
Schneer, starring Kerwin Mathews and filmed in SUPER-DYNAMATION for
Columbia Pictures release." Special effects by Ray Harryhausen. Back cover
shows line-drawing artwork of Gulliver fastened to ground (also not from
the movie).

Gulliver's Travels see *The 3 Worlds of Gulliver*

The Hammer Horror Omnibus. By John Burke. London: Pan Books Ltd.,
   1966. No. X520.
   Novelizations of four movies, with colored artwork from each on front
and back covers: *The Gorgon; The Curse of Frankenstein; The Revenge of
Frankenstein;* and *The Curse of the Mummy's Tomb.*

The Hammer Horror Film Omnibus. By John Burke. London: Pan Books,
   1966; Third Printing, 1975.
   Similar to above (same four novelizations) but with different cover: color
artwork of Peter Cushing surrounded by snakes.

Hangover Square. By Patrick Hamilton. Cleveland and New York: The
   World Publishing Company, Third Printing, April 1945.
   Dust jacket (only) front cover shows Laird Cregar and Linda Darnell;
back cover has four photos from the 20th Century–Fox movie.

The Haunted Strangler. By John C. Cooper. New York: Ace Books, Inc., c.
   1958. No. D-359.
   Front cover has drawing of Boris Karloff; back cover has photo of Karloff
from the MLC/Producers Associates film.

The Haunting of Hill House. By Shirley Jackson. New York: Popular Library,
   June 1962. No. K6.

Front and back covers have b&w photos of Julie Harris and Claire Bloom from the MGM film.

Having Wonderful Crime. By Craig Rice. Cleveland and New York: The World Publishing Company, c. 1943; third printing, March 1945.
  Dust jacket (only) has two black and white photos from the RKO mystery/comedy with Pat O'Brien, Carole Landis, and George Murphy.

He Who Gets Slapped. By George A. Carlin. New York: Grosset & Dunlap, c. 1925.
  Eight photos from the 1924 MGM film with Lon Chaney. The note page after the dedication states: "The motion picture upon which this novel is based was made from Gregory Zilboorg's translation of Andreyev's play produced by The Theatre Guild." Dust jacket has color artwork showing Lon Chaney and Norma Shearer.

He Who Gets Slapped: A Play in Four Acts. By Leonid Andreyev. Translated from Russian with an Introduction by Gregory Zilboorg. New York: Brentano's, 1922; Third Printing, February 1923.
  Frontispiece photo of a scene from the Theatre Guild stage production.

Headed for a Hearse. By Jonathan Latimer. Garden City, N.Y.: The Sun Dial Press, 1937.
  A list of characters and actors, headed by a photo of Preston Foster as Detective Crane, is followed by a double-title-page montage of photos from the Universal Pictures movie. The title page reads, "*The Westland Case: Photoplay Title of Headed for a Hearse.*" (*Headed for a Hearse* appears on the spine.)

Histoires Extraordinaires see *Fantastic Tales*

"Hold That Ghost." Fictionized by Sylvia Marks. In: *Screen Romances*, Vol. 25, No. 148 (September 1941), 42, 67–68.
  One photo plus ghost drawing; photo shows Joan Davis, Evelyn Ankers, Bud Abbott, Richard Carlson, and Lou Costello from the Universal film.

"Hold That Ghost." In: *Movie Story Magazine*, Vol. 16, No. 89 (September 1941), 35, 52–56.
  One photo from the Universal Picture with Abbott and Costello, Richard Carlson, Joan Davis, and Evelyn Ankers.

Home Sweet Homicide. By Craig Rice. Cleveland and New York: The World Publishing Company, 1946.

Dust jacket has six pictures from the 20th Century–Fox movie with Peggy Ann Garner, Randolph Scott, and Lynn Bari.

"Horror by Night." By Ian Conyers. In: *Film Weekly*, Vol. 5, No. 132 (April 25, 1931), 23–24.
Two photos from the Universal film *The Cat Creeps*, plus a photo of Helen Twelvetrees on the front cover of the magazine. Block on page 23 reads, "A Gripping Short Story of weird happenings in a lonely house." Note at end of story says, "This story is based on incidents in the Universal film, 'The Cat Creeps,' with Helen Twelvetrees as Annabelle, Raymond Hackett as Paul, and Jean Hersholt as the doctor, released next Monday." (The plot of this fictionization is quite different from that in the contemporary *Boy's Cinema* version.)

The Hound of the Baskervilles. By A. Conan Doyle. "The G. Washington Edition." New York: Doubleday, Doran & Company, Inc., c. 1901, 1902, 1930.
Frontispiece is b&w photo of "Mr. Richard Gordon, who plays the title role in the radio dramatization of Sherlock Holmes." Gordon wears deerstalker and holds pipe. Title page and front cover have silhouette of Holmes, in a circle.

The Hound of the Baskervilles. By A. Conan Doyle. New York: Grosset & Dunlap, "Published March, 1902, R, Fonrth [*sic*] Impression."
"A Special Limited Edition." Eight Sidney Paget illustrations. Front cover has photograph of William Gillette, with pipe, as Holmes.

"The Hound of the Baskervilles." Fictionized by Charles MacGregor. In: *Screen Romances*, Vol. 18, No. 120 (May 1939), 36–39, 79–80.
Seven photos from the 20th Century–Fox film with Basil Rathbone, Nigel Bruce, Richard Greene, Lionel Atwill, and John Carradine.

"The House of Dracula." In: *Movie Story Magazine*, Vol. 20, No. 141 (January 1946), 54–55, 94–97.
Two photos from Universal film with John Carradine, Lon Chaney, Martha O'Driscoll, Glenn Strange, "Poni Adams" (Jane Adams), Onslow Stevens, Lionel Atwill, and Ludwig Stossel. Carradine is shown with spread cape; Chaney and O'Driscoll appear together. Page 94 adds a one-column article, "On the Set of The House of Dracula," showing an additional photo of make-up man Jack Pierce applying Frankenstein make-up to Lon Chaney in *Ghost of Frankenstein*. (The same issue has "The Falcon's Alibi" and "The Spider.")

"The House of Mystery." In: *Boy's Cinema*, 769 (September 8, 1934), 13–20, 25.

"The creeping horror of a half seen horrible Presence metes out death to one by one of the members of a sinister house party at the secluded country mansion of John Prenn, crippled and eccentric philanthropist. Starring Ed Lowry and Verna Hillie." Six photos from the Pathé Pictures film; credits on page 2. Three of the photos show the gorilla from this classic old house thriller. (The same issue has Episode 8 of "Vanishing Shadow.")

The House of Peril. By Mrs. Bellow Lowndes. London: The Readers Library Publishing Company Ltd., n.d. No. 261.

Dust jacket (only) has color artwork on front cover showing two young women in 1920s dress reacting to something being pointed out by old woman fortune teller, with crystal ball and cards. Back cover has b&w artwork showing young woman in 1920s dress being menaced, on a stairway, by a heavy set woman below and a clenched-fisted man above. Editor's Note says, "In 1919 the story was dramatized by Horace Annesley Vachell, and, with a notable cast including Owen Nares, Norman McKinnel, Miss Brooke, Stella Rho, and Annie Schletter, enjoyed a run of several months at the Queen's Theatre in London. The title of the play was also altered [from *The Chink in the Armour*] to *The House of Peril*. This title was also adopted when in 1922 the Astra Company produced a five-reel film of the story, in which Fay Compton played the heroine." Dust jacket artwork is probably from the film version.

"The House of Rothschild." Fictionized by Ethel M. Pomeroy. In: *Screen Romances*, Vol. 10, No. 60 (May 1934), 12–21, 106.

Ten photos from the 1935 20th Century picture with George Arliss, Boris Karloff, and Loretta Young. Karloff appears in two of them.

House of Rothschild see *The Rise of the House of Rothschild*

The House of the Seven Gables. By Nathaniel Hawthorne. Cleveland, Ohio & New York, N.Y.: The World Publishing Co., 1937.

Dust jacket (only) has one b&w photo of George Sanders, Vincent Price, and Margaret Lindsay from the 1940 Universal film.

The House of the Seven Gables see *Nathaniel Hawthorne's Twice Told Tales* (comic book)

The Hunchback of Notre Dame. By Victor Hugo. New York: A. L. Burt, n.d.

Four photos from the 1923 Universal film with Lon Chaney. The dust jacket has a colored photo of Patsy Ruth Miller.

The Hunchback of Notre Dame. By Victor Hugo. New York: Grosset & Dunlap, n.d.

Dust jacket (only) has four photos from the 1939 RKO Radio film with Charles Laughton.

The Hunchback of Notre Dame. By Victor Hugo. Philadelphia: Macrae-Smith Company, n.d.

Eight photos from the 1939 RKO Radio film with Charles Laughton. (This copy is enhanced by a previous owner's having tipped in the four Lon Chaney movie photos, too.)

The Hunchback of Notre Dame. By Victor Hugo. London and Glasgow: Collins, n.d. Library of Classics.

Seven photos from the 1939 RKO film with Charles Laughton.

The Hunchback of Notre Dame. Original Screen Version By Perely [*sic*] Poore Sheehan. New York: George D. Swarz & Company, 1923.

This 141 page adaptation of the Victor Hugo story is a novelization of the 1923 film; it has four photos, one showing Lon Chaney on the wheel, with Patsy Ruth Miller. Front cover says, "An Original Motion Picture Edition"; the cover correctly spells author's name as "Perley" while the title page reads "Perely."

"The Hunchback of Notre Dame." Told in Short-Story Form by Janet Reid. In: *The Motion Picture Magazine* (1923), 53–57, 98–100.

Seven photos from the Universal version with Lon Chaney. (Cover and first 25 pages missing from this copy.)

The Hunchback of Notre Dame. By Victor Hugo. New York: Dodd, Mead & Company, 1939.

Sixteen photos from the 1939 RKO Radio film with Charles Laughton.

"The Hunchback of Notre Dame." In: *Screen Book Magazine*, Vol. 22, No. 5 (December 1939), 35–37.

Nine photos from the RKO film with Charles Laughton and Maureen O'Hara, with captions briefly giving the film's story. A tenth photo, on the first page, is of Lon Chaney in the role. None of the pictures show Laughton's facial makeup.

The Hunchback of Notre Dame. By Victor Hugo. New York: Triangle Books, 1940.

Front cover of dust jacket (only) has photos from the 1939 RKO Radio film with Charles Laughton.

"The Hunchback of Notre Dame." Fictionized by Jean Francis Webb. In:
Screen Romances, Vol. 18, No. 129 (February 1940), 51–58, 60, 62.
Ten photos from 1939 RKO Radio production with Charles Laughton,
Maureen O'Hara, Sir Cedric Hardwicke, Thomas Mitchell, and Edmund
O'Brien. (The same issue has "Raffles.")

"The Hunchback of Notre Dame." In: *Movie Story Magazine*, Vol. 14, No.
70 (February 1940), 43, 74.
One photo from the 1939 RKO Radio film with Charles Laughton and
Maureen O'Hara.

Hunchback of Notre Dame. By Victor Hugo. New York: Avon Publications,
Inc., c. 1957. No. T-190.
Front cover has color photo of Gina Lollobrigida and b&w photo of
Anthony Quinn from the Allied Artists film; back cover has red-tinted
photo of both. Twenty-three b&w photos appear throughout the text.

The Hunchback of Notre Dame. Dell comic No. 854. New York: Dell Publishing Co., Inc., 1957.
Comic book version of the 1957 Allied Artists film with Anthony Quinn.
Front cover has color photo; inside front cover has seven b&w photos, and
film credits.

"The Hunchback of Notre Dame." Adapted by Jean Francis Webb. In:
Screen Stories, Vol. 60, No. 12 (December 1961), 56–59, 66–71.
Reprint of story originally published in *Screen Romances* (February 1940);
this version has three pictures, different from those in original printing, from
the Charles Laughton/Maureen O'Hara RKO Radio version.

"I Married a Witch." In: *Movie Story Magazine*, Vol. 14, No. 105 (January
1943), 26–29, 85–86, 88.
Five photos, and one portrait photo of Fredric March, from the United
Artists film with March, Veronica Lake, Robert Benchley, Susan Hayward,
and Cecil Kellaway. (The same issue has "The Cat People" and "One Dangerous Night.")

"I Walked with a Zombie." In: *Movie Story Magazine*, Vol. 15, No. 109
(May 1943), 34–35, 41–43, 45–48.
Two photos from the 1943 Val Lewton RKO-Radio picture. (The same
issue has "Lady of Burlesque.")

The Illustrated Dracula. By Bram Stoker. New York: Drake Publishers Inc.,
1975.

Numerous b&w photos, mainly from Lugosi screen and stage versions, with a few photos from the Hammer *Curse of Dracula.*

"The Innocents." Adapted by Jean Francis Webb. In: *Screen Stories,* Vol. 61, No. 3 (March 1962), 14–16, 58–61.
Three photos from the 20th Century–Fox film with Deborah Kerr.

Insidious Dr. Fu Manchu. By Sax Rohmer. New York: A. L. Burt Company, c. 1913, 5th printing 1920.
Four photos from the 1929 Paramount film *Mysterious Dr. Fu Manchu* with Warner Oland and Jean Arthur.

Interference. By Roland Pertwee. New York: Grosset & Dunlap, c. 1927.
Eight photos from the 1929 Paramount film with William Powell. Dust jacket has colored picture of Evelyn Brent from the movie.

"Invisible Agent." Fictionized by Helen Cunningham. In: *Screen Romances,* Vol. 27, No. 160 (September 1942), 32–34, 82–84.
Six photos from the Universal film with Jon Hall, Ilona Massey, Peter Lorre, Sir Cedric Hardwicke, J. Edward Bromberg, and Lionel Atwill. Credits given on page 32. Lorre appears in photo on page 32.

The Invisible Man. By H. G. Wells. New York: Grosset & Dunlap, c. 1897.
Both endpapers have photos from the 1933 Universal film with Claude Rains. The dust jacket has colored scenes from the movie on its front; the back lists thirteen other photoplay editions and shows ten small photos, including one of Boris Karloff in *The Old Dark House.*

"Invisible Man's Revenge." Fictionized by Jane MacDonald. In: *Silver Screen,* Vol. 14, No. 9 (July 1944), 48–49, 81–85.
"The incredible story of a maniac, with sinister powers, seeking a fortune he claims to be his." Four photos from the Universal film with Jon Hall, Evelyn Ankers, John Carradine, and Gale Sondergaard.

"The Invisible Woman." Fictionized by Helen McCloy. In: *Screen Romances,* Vol. 24, No. 141 (February 1941), 43–44, 68–70.
Four photos from the Universal film with Virginia Bruce, John Howard, and John Barrymore.

Island at the Top of the World. By Ian Cameron. New York: Avon Books, 1961. No. 20966.
Front cover has color poster art from the Walt Disney movie; back cover has six color photos.

Island at the Top of the World. By Ian Cameron. New York: William Morrow & Company, Inc., c. 1961; published in U.S., 1968.
Dust jacket has four photos and poster illustrations from the 1974 Walt Disney movie.

Island of Dr. Moreau. By H. G. Wells. New York City: Duffield and Green, c. 1932.
Three photos from the 1932 Paramount movie *Island of Lost Souls*, with Charles Laughton. (Bela Lugosi does not appear in these photos.)

Island of Dr. Moreau. By H. G. Wells.; and a novelization of the screenplay by Joseph Silva. Garden City, N.Y.: Nelson Doubleday, Inc., c. 1977.
Two versions of the same story in one book, illustrated with twenty-two photos from 1977 American-International film with Burt Lancaster and Michael York. Dust jacket has nine additional color photos.

Jack the Giant Killer. Dell Movie Classic comic No. 12-374-301. New York: Dell Publishing Co., Inc., 1962.
Front cover has color artwork from film, of Jack hanging from the talon of a flying dragon monster. Inside front cover has six b&w photos from the United Artists movie, including three of villain Torin Thatcher and two of Kerwin Mathews, and film credits.

Jack the Ripper. By Stuart James. Based on the original screenplay by Jimmy Sangster. Plus Bill Doll's factual account of the actual "Ripper" murders. Derby, Connecticut: Monarch Books, 1960. No. 143.
Front cover has color drawing of woman being threatened by a knife-wielding assailant. Back cover has blue tinted photo from the Joseph E. Levine/Embassy Release motion picture. Back cover has note: "I saw Joe Levine's JACK THE RIPPER. It's not for kiddies or even beatniks. The latter might be so scared they'd go to work!"—HEDDA HOPPER.

Jack the Ripper. By Stuart James. Based on the original screenplay by Jimmie Sangster. Plus Bill Doll's factual account of the actual "Ripper" murders—the most infamous series of unsolved crimes in the history of Scotland Yard. JACK THE RIPPER, a Joseph E. Levine motion picture presentation—An Embassy Release. New York: Frederick Fell, Inc., Publishers, 1960.
Harcover edition of the more famous Monarch paperback. Dust jacket has artwork of Ripper figure holding knife over prostrate prostitute; her lips, only, are red in otherwise b&w drawing. Doll's account, "The Crime de la Crime," is a background article on the production of the 1959 film,

with quotes from producer Joseph E. Levine and an extended quotation from an article by Alan Hynd in *True Magazine* of 1956, asserting that the Ripper was a Spaniard named Alonzo Maduro.

Jamaica Inn see *Modern Mystery and Adventure Novels*

Jason and the Argonauts. Dell Movie classic comic No. 12–376–310. New York, N.Y.: Dell Publishing Co., Inc., August–October, 1963.
   Comic book version. Front cover has color photo of Triton holding apart the Clashing Rocks, from the 1963 Columbia Pictures movie. Inside front cover has four b&w photos and movie credits. Special effects by Ray Harryhausen.

A Journey to the Center of the Earth. By Jules Verne. New York: Permabooks, 1st printing, September 1959. No. M 4161.
   Front cover has two color photos from the 20th Century–Fox movie with James Mason, Pat Boone, Arlene Dahl, and Diane Baker.

"A Journey to the Center of the Earth." Adapted by Jean Francis Webb. In: *Screen Stories*, Vol. 58, No. 11 (December 1959), 44–46, 82–85.
   Four photos from the 1959 20th Century–Fox film with Pat Boone, James Mason, and Arlene Dahl.

Jules Verne's Master of the World (Including Robur the Conqueror). New York: Ace Books, Inc., n.d. (Note says text taken from 1951 hardcover edition.) No. D-504.
   Front cover has two color pictures from the 1961 American-International film with Vincent Price.

The Kennel Murder Case. By S. S. Van Dine. With a new introduction by Chris Steinbrunner. Boston, Mass.: Gregg Press, 1980 reprint of 1933 edition.
   Eight photos from the 1933 Warner Bros. film with William Powell as Philo Vance.

"The Kennel Murder Case." Fictionized by Morton Savell. In: *Screen Romances*, Vol. 10, No. 56 (January 1934), 74–78, 92, 94, 96.
   Seven photos from Warner Bros. picture with William Powell as Philo Vance, Mary Astor, Eugene Pallette, and Ralph Morgan. (The same issue has "Tarzan and His Mate.")

"The Kennel Murder Case." In: *Boy's Cinema*, No. 738 (February 3, 1934), 7–16, 23–25.

"When Archer Coe was found dead in a room bolted on the inside, the police concluded that he had committed suicide. As a result of Philo Vance's investigations, however, seven people speedily became suspected of murder, and the solution of the mystery provided the famous detective with the biggest case of his career." Nine photos from the Warner Bros. mystery with William Powell as Philo Vance, Mary Astor, Eugene Pallette, and Ralph Morgan. Credits on page 27. (The same issue has Episode 1 of "The Perils of Pauline.")

The Kennel Murder Case see *Philo Vance Murder Cases*

King Kong. Novelization by Delos W. Lovelace. New York: Grosset & Dunlap, c. 1932.
  Endpapers (only) have twelve photos from the 1933 RKO Radio movie. Color dust jacket has artwork front cover portraying Kong holding brunette in one hand while mangling airplane in other hand; dinosaurs in background, cityscape with Chrysler Building in foreground. Spine has b&w drawing of Kong in a cage; back cover is color portrayal of Kong fighting tyrannosaurus, ripping its bloody mouth. Semi-nude brunette rests on ground at their feet. Special effects by Willis O'Brien.

King Kong. By Edgar Wallace and Merian C. Cooper, novelization by Delos W. Lovelace. New York: Bantam Books, October 1965. No. F3093.
  "Never before in paperback" edition; front cover has color artwork of Kong and Fay Wray from the RKO Radio movie.

"The King Murder." In: *The Film Star Weekly*, Vol. 3, No. 55 (December 9, 1933), 17–21.
  Two photos from the "baffling murder mystery" from Universal, with Conway Tearle and Natalie Moorehead.

King of the Jungle: Photoplay Title of The Lion's Way. By C. T. Stoneham. New York: Grosset & Dunlap, 1932.
  Four photos from the 1933 Paramount movie with Buster Crabbe.

King Solomon's Mines. Based on the novel by H. Rider Haggard. London and Melbourne: Ward, Locke & Co., Limited, n.d.
  Eight color plates and eighty photographs from the 1950 MGM movie with Stewart Granger and Deborah Kerr. Dust jacket has two color photos.

King Solomon's Mines. Fictionized by Jean Francis Webb; based on the story by H. Rider Haggard. New York: Dell Publishing Co., 1950. No. 433.

Map-back paperback with one photo from the MGM Stewart Granger/ Deborah Kerr movie on front. (Story not the same as the hardcover cited above.)

"King Solomon's Mines." In: *Movie Story Magazine*, Vol. 30, No. 200 (December 1950), 30–33, 70–74.
Seven photos, one tinted red, from the MGM Picture with Stewart Granger and Deborah Kerr.

Konga. By Dean Owen. Based on an original story and screenplay by Aben Kandel and Herman Cohen. Derby, Connecticut: Monarch Books, Inc., 1960. No. MM604.
Front cover has color drawing of a huge gorilla reaching for man assaulting a blonde woman; back cover reproduces gorilla portion, tinted green. Tied to the American-International film.

The Lady in the Lake. By Raymond Chandler. New York: Grosset & Dunlap, 1943.
Dust jacket (only) has photos from 1946 MGM film with Robert Montgomery as Philip Marlowe. Front shows overlapping faces of Montgomery, Audrey Totter, and Lloyd Nolan; back cover shows same three in one still; spine shows Montgomery reading a newspaper. Inside flaps give mini-sketches of five characters, with photos of each (adding characters played by Leon Ames and Jayne Meadows).

Lady in the Morgue. By Jonathan Latimer. Garden City, N.Y.: The Crime Club, Inc., by Doubleday, Doran & Co., Inc., 1936.
Dust jacket (only) has one b&w photo of Preston Foster, Frank Jenks, and Patricia Ellis from the 1938 Universal movie; the three are looking down at a drawing of a reclining female corpse. A smaller image of the same corpse appears on the spine of the dust jacket and of the book itself.

Lady of Burlesque: Originally published as The G-String Murders. By Gypsy Rose Lee. Cleveland and New York: The World Publishing Company, c. 1941; Tower Books Edition fifth printing, April 1943.
Dust jacket has seven photos from the 1943 United Artists film *Lady of Burlesque* with Barbara Stanwyck. Back cover of jacket (five photos) is the same as that on *G-String Murders* copy (above). Front cover photo here is much larger, and there is an additional photo on the jacket spine.

"Lady of Burlesque." In: *Movie Story Magazine*, Vol. 15, No. 109 (May 1943), 24–25, 75.

Five photos and one behind-the-scenes photo from the 1943 United Artists picture with Barbara Stanwyck. (The same issue has "I Walked with a Zombie.")

Lady of Burlesque see *The G-String Murders*

"The Lady Vanishes." Fictionized by Herbert Kaufman. In: *Screen Romances*, 18, 115 (December 1938), 64–67, 105–106.
Seven photos from the 1938 Gaumont film directed by Alfred Hitchcock; credits on page 65. (The same issue has "Devil's Island.")

The Land That Time Forgot. By Edgar Rice Burroughs. Garden City, N.Y.: Nelson Doubleday, Inc., c. 1918, 1945, 1946.
Book club edition with six photos from the 1975 American-International release with Doug McClure; dust jacket includes color artwork based on movie scenes. The volume includes two additional stories, *The People That Time Forgot* and *Out of Time's Abyss*.

The Land That Time Forgot. By Edgar Rice Burroughs. New York: Ace Books, c. 1918. No. 47023.
Front cover has color artwork from the American-International film with Doug McClure; back cover has five color photos.

The Land Unknown. Dell Movie Classic comic No. 845. New York: Dell Publishing Co., Inc., 1957.
Comic book has color artwork on front cover with prominent red tyrannosaurus; note says, "A Universal-International Picture Photographed in Cinemascope." Inside front cover has four b&w photos from the movie with Jock Mahoney, and Shawn Smith; one shows a tyrannosaurus in a swamp. Inside cover also lists film credits.

"The Last Days of Pompeii." In: *Boy's Cinema*, No. 850 (March 28, 1936), 2–12, 25–27.
"When Marcus the Blacksmith loses his wife and little son, money becomes his god, and first as a gladiator, then as a slave-dealer, he amasses a fortune. But his adopted son, Flavius, grows up to throw in his lot with the slaves—and so incurs the penalty of death. A tremendous drama of a bygone age, starring Preston Foster." Included here because its special effects were done by Willis O'Brien. Cover montage and six photos from the 1935 RKO Radio Pictures film starring Foster and Basil Rathbone. (The same issue has "The Spanish Cape Mystery.")

The Last Warning. By Wadsworth Camp. London: The Readers Library
   Publishing Company Ltd., n.d. No. 264.
   Illustrated with eight photos on four double-sided sheets from the 1929 Universal silent film with Laura La Plante and John Bowles, a follow-up to *The
Cat and the Canary* directed by Paul Leni (his last film). Dust jacket has color
drawing of La Plante on front; on back, colored drawing of Torben Meyer on
staircase looking at giant skeletal hand. (According to *Golden Horrors*, the
novel by Camp was originally published as *Backstage Phantom* in 1916.)

"Laugh, Clown, Laugh." In: *Picture Show*, Vol. 21, No. 539 (August 31,
   1929), 6–8.
   "A Poignant Drama of Sorrow behind 'A Painted Laugh.'" Cover and
two internal photos from the MGM film with Lon Chaney and Loretta
Young.

"The Laurel-Hardy Murder Mystery." In: *Boy's Cinema*, No. 586 (March
   7, 1931), 10–14, 27.
   "Two down-and-outs come to claim a huge fortune but find themselves
suspected of a crime and forced to stay the night in a haunted house. Starring Stan Laurel and Oliver Hardy." Five photos from the MGM mystery
comedy.

"The Leopard Man." In: *Movie Story Magazine*, Vol. 15, No. 112 (August
   1943), 42, 57–60, 62–64.
   Four photos from the 1943 RKO Radio Picture produced by Val Lewton and directed by Jacques Tourneur.

"The List of Adrian Messenger." Adapted by Jean Francis Webb. In: *Screen
   Stories*, Vol. 62, No. 6 (June 1963), 26–29, 68–71.
   Ten photos from the Universal mystery directed by John Huston, with
George C. Scott. (None of the "mystery guest" makeups are shown.)

The Little Sister see *Marlowe*

The Lodger. By Mrs. Belloc Lowndes. London: The Readers Library Pub-
   lishing Company Ltd., n.d. No. 185.
   This copy is without dust jacket; no internal illustrations. The "Editor's
Note," however, does refer to the 1926 Gainsborough film version with Ivor
Novello "now being released."

The Lodger. By Marie Belloc Lowndes. Cleveland and New York: The
   World Publishing Company, 1944.

Dust jacket has seven photos from the 20th Century–Fox film with Laird Cregar.

"The Lodger." In: *Movie Story Magazine*, Vol. 16, No. 118 (February 1944), 40–41, 63–71.
Five photos from 20th Century–Fox film, directed by John Brahm, with Merle Oberon, George Sanders, Laird Cregar; credits on page 40. (The same issue has "Curse of the Cat People.")

Lola. By Owen Davis. New York: Grosset & Dunlap, c. 1915.
Sixteen photos from The World Film Corporation's 1916 picture with Clara Kimball Young. (Dead daughter of doctor who invented life-restoring machine is revived.) Film credits given opposite page 1 include Lionel Belmore, whose photo appears opposite page 282. (Belmore would go on to play the Burgomaster in both *Frankenstein* and *Son of Frankenstein*.)

London After Midnight. By Marie Coolidge-Rask. Based on the Scenario of the Tod Browning Production. London: The Readers Library Publishing Company Ltd., n.d. [No. 228].
Eight photos from 1927 MGM Lon Chaney film; only one photo the same as in the Grosset & Dunlap edition. Dust jacket has color artwork on front and back. Front shows woman menaced by beaver-hat man in front and bat-winged woman behind; back shows man's face peering into window with vampire-like figure hiding to the side.

London After Midnight. By Marie Coolidge-Rask. Based on the Scenario of the Tod Browning Production. New York: Grosset & Dunlap, 1928.
Eight photos from the lost 1927 MGM film with Lon Chaney.

London After Midnight see "The Mark of the Vampire"

The Lone Wolf. By Louis Joseph Vance. New York: A. L. Burt Company, c. 1914.
Three photos from the 1924 Associated Exhibitors version with Jack Holt as the title character, and Gustav von Seyffertitz (photo opposite page 230).

The Lone Wolf see also "One Dangerous Night"

The Lone Wolf Returns. By Louis Joseph Vance. New York: Grosset & Dunlap, 1923.
Eight photos from the 1926 Columbia movie with Bert Lytell. Dust jacket has color drawing of scene from the movie.

"The Lone Wolf Returns." In: *Boy's Cinema*, No. 861 (June 13, 1936), cover
   and 2–12, 26–27.
   "Evading the police after a jewel robbery, Michael Lanyard, alias 'The
Lone Wolf,' mingles with the guests of an heiress next door, named Marcia Stewart. He falls in love with the girl and resolves to go straight; but
other jewel thieves involve him in the theft of Marcia's emeralds—and a
very clever detective is called in to run him down. A gay, yet thrilling, mystery drama, starring Melvyn Douglas and Gail Patrick." Eight photos
(including cover) from the Columbia Pictures production. (The same issue
has Episode 6, "Flaming Torture," of *Flash Gordon*.)

Look Magazine—"Son of Frankenstein."

The Lost City. Fictionized by Charles Reed Jones. New York: Engle-van
   Wiseman, Book Corporations, c. 1935.
   A "Five Star Library" book, similar in format to Big Little Books. Front and
back covers have color artwork from 1935 S. S. Krellbert serial with William
(Stage) Boyd, Kane Richmond, and Claudia Dell; 61 internal b&w photos.

The Lost Continent. By Dennis Wheatley. London: Arrow Books, 1968. No.
   062.
   Front and back covers have color photos from Hammer Film Production with Eric Porter and Hildegard Knef. Cover reads "*Uncharted Seas Now
Filmed as The Lost Continent*"; title page reads *Uncharted Seas.*

Lost Horizon. By James Hilton. New York: Grosset & Dunlap, c. 1936.
   Endpapers have photo from the 1937 Columbia movie with Ronald Colman. Dust jacket has artwork rendering of Tibetan monastery, but not from
the movie.

The Lost Patrol. From The Story "Patrol" By Philip MacDonald. Adapted
   By Kenneth Hallam. Racine, Wisconsin: Whitman Publishing Company, c. 1934.
   Big Little Book version of the RKO Picture starring Victor McLaglen,
Boris Karloff, Wallace Ford, Reginald Denny, Sammy Stein, and Alan Hale,
directed by John Ford; Merian C. Cooper, executive producer. Seventy-
five b&w photos, plus two more color photos on front and back covers. The
first of many photos of Karloff as "Sanders, the Religious Fanatic," appears
opposite page 12.

The Lost World. By A. Conan Doyle. New York: A. L. Burt, c. 1912.
   Four photos from the 1925 First National movie (frontispiece of two

dinosaurs), plus additional colored photo on dust jacket. Special effects by Willis O'Brien.

The Lost World. [Sheet Music] Words by Harry B. Smith. Music by Rudolf Friml. New York: Henry Watterson, Inc., c. 1924.

Organ copy sheet music, with ukulele arrangement, for song "Inspired by the wealth of romance in the impressive photoplay 'The Lost World'." No illustrations.

"The Lost World." Fictionized by Patricia Cork Dugan. In: *Motion Picture Classic*, 20, 5 (January 1925), 27–30, 89–90.

Six photos from the First National film with Wallace Beery, Bessie Love, and Lewis Stone. One photo shows Bull Montana in apeman makeup; none show dinosaurs. Credits on page 29.

The Lost World. Dell Movie Classic comic No. 1145. New York: Dell Publishing Co., Inc., 1960.

Comic book has color photos on cover from Irwin Allen production with Claude Rains, Fernando Lamas, and Michael Rennie. Inside front cover has five b&w photos and film credits.

Lust for a Vampire. By William Hughes. London: Sphere Books Ltd., 1971. No. 42633.

Front cover has color photo from the 1971 Hammer film.

MacKenna's Gold. By Will Henry. New York: Bantam Books, May 1969, 2nd printing. No. S4361.

Front cover has color artwork of seven recognizable characters from the Columbia movie; back cover has thirteen b&w photos of faces of characters. Story is a kind of H. Rider Haggard quest for a lost valley and treasure, set in the U.S. West.

"The Mad Ghoul." In: *Movie Story Magazine*, Vol. 16, No. 116 (December 1943), 44, 71–77.

Four photos from the Universal film with David Bruce, Evelyn Ankers, George Zucco, and Turhan Bey.

"Mad Love." Fictionized by Margaret Mahin. In: *Screen Romances*, Vol. 13, No. 76 (September, 1935), 34–36, 106–108.

Four photos from the MGM film with Peter Lorre, Frances Drake, and Colin Clive.

Mad Monster Party. Dell comic No. 12–460–801. New York: Dell Publishing Co., 1967.
Cover has three color photos from the Rankin-Bass animated film featuring the voice of Boris Karloff. Inside front cover has three additional b&w photos.

Madhouse. By Angus Hall. London: Sphere Books Limited, 1969; reprinted September 1970. No. 0 7221 4272 2.
Front cover reads "Devilday now filmed as Madhouse"; title page says *Devilday.* Front cover has color picture of "Vincent Price as Paul Toombs." Credits for the American International & Amicus Films release starring Price, Peter Cushing, and Robert Quarry are given on the back cover.

"The Maltese Falcon." Fictionized by Helen McCloy. In: *Screen Romances*, Vol. 25, No. 149 (October 1941), 30–32, 80–82; credits on p. 17.
Five photos showing Humphrey Bogart, Sidney Greenstreet, Mary Astor, Peter Lorre, Elisha Cook, Jr., and Jerome Cowan from the MGM film.

The Man Who Could Cheat Death. By Barre Lyndon and Jimmie Sangster. New York: Avon Book Division, The Hearst Corporation, 1959. No. T-362.
Front cover has half-green, half-red photo of creature from the 1959 Hammer film with Anton Diffring, Hazel Court, and Christopher Lee. Back cover has yellow-tinted photo of Diffring character holding his hand over the mouth of a woman to stop her from screaming. Film credits are given opposite title page.

"The Man Who Knew Too Much." Fictionized by Margaret E. Mahin. In: *Screen Romances*, Vol. 12, No. 68 (January 1935), 83–85, 92–93.
Four photos from the Gaumont-British film by Alfred Hitchcock, with Leslie Banks and Peter Lorre. (The same issue has "The Man Who Reclaimed His Head.")

The Man Who Laughs. By Victor Hugo. New York: Grosset & Dunlap, n.d. Hardcover.
Eight photos from the 1928 Universal movie with Conrad Veidt and Mary Philbin.

The Man Who Laughs. By Victor Hugo. Abridged by Metcalfe Wood. London: The Readers Library Publishing Company Ltd., n.d. [No. 211].
Illustrated with eight photos on four double-side pages from the 1928 Universal movie with Conrad Veidt and Mary Philbin. Dust jacket has

color drawing of Veidt/Gwynplaine on front; back has color drawing of man peering from behind red curtain that he pulls aside.

The Man Who Laughs: Based on the Motion Picture Story. By Paul Gulick. New York: Jacobsen-Hodgkinson Corporation, c. 1928. Paperback.
Front cover has color-tinted photo of Conrad Veidt and Mary Philbin from the 1928 Universal movie. Back cover has two more b&w photos; eight additional photos printed within the text.

"The Man Who Laughs." By Felix Orman. In: *Screen Book*, No. 2 (September 1928), 50–57.
Six photos from the Universal film with Conrad Veidt and Mary Philbin.

"The Man Who Reclaimed His Head." Fictionized by Mary Chadbourne-Brown. In: *Screen Romances*, Vol. 12, No. 68 (January 1935), 46–48, 104.
Four photos from Universal film with Claude Rains, Lionel Atwill, Joan Bennett, and Wallace Ford. (The same issue has "The Man Who Knew Too Much.")

"The Man Who Reclaimed His Head." In: *Screen Stories*, No. 276 (May 18, 1935), 3–14, 34–35.
"Kept at the front by a man who is seeking to steal his wife, a soldier returns, and vengeance is his." Cover plus five photos from Universal film with Claude Rains, Joan Bennett, Lionel Atwill, and Wallace Ford.

"The Mandarin Mystery." Fictionized by Mary Chadbourne. In: *Screen Romances*, Vol. 16, No. 93 (February 1937), 74–77.
Four photos from the Republic picture with Eddie Quillan as Ellery Queen. (The same issue has "After the Thin Man.")

"The Mark of the Vampire." Fictionized by Edwin V. Burkholder. In: *Screen Romances*, Vol. 12, No. 73 (June 1935), 64–67, 92–93.
Five photos from 1935 MGM horror classic with Bela Lugosi, Lionel Barrymore, Carol Borland (here listed as "Vorland"), Lionel Atwill, and Jean Hersholt. Lugosi and Borland appear on page 66, Borland again on 67. This is a remake of Lon Chaney's *London After Midnight*. (The same issue has "The Case of the Curious Bride.")

"The Mark of the Vampire." In: *Boy's Cinema*, No. 813 (July 13, 1935), 9–14, 30.
"The villagers think that the district is haunted by ghosts. The owner of the castle dies and on his neck are the marks of a vampire, and, a year later,

a young man nearly dies from a similar attack. An Inspector of Police and a Professor of Criminology attempt to solve the mystery. Starring Lionel Barrymore, Lionel Atwill and Bela Lugosi." Four photos (two with Lugosi) from the 1935 MGM film, also starring Jean Hersholt, Carol Borland, and Donald Meek. Credits on page 2.

Marlowe. (Original Title: *The Little Sister*). By Raymond Chandler. Richmond Hill, Ontario: Simon & Schuster of Canada, Ltd., Sixth Printing, August 1969. No. 75434.
   Paperback with one photo on front cover of James Garner and Rita Moreno from the MGM film; credits on back cover.

Mask of Demetrios see *A Coffin for Demetrios*

"The Mask of Fu Manchu." In: *The Film Star Weekly*, Vol. 1, No. 18, (March 25, 1933), 27.
   One-page plot summary, with two photos and film credits, of the 1932 MGM film with Boris Karloff, Lewis Stone, Karen Morley, Jean Hersholt, and Myrna Loy.

Masque of the Red Death. Adapted by Elsie Lee from the screenplay by R. Wright Campbell. New York: Lancer Books, 1964. No. 72–725.
   Front and back covers have five photos from the 1964 American-International movie with Vincent Price.

Masque of the Red Death. Dell Movie Classic comic No. 12–490–410. New York: Dell Publishing Co., Inc., 1964.
   Comic book version. Front cover has two overlapping color photos from the 1964 American-International picture; inside front cover has five b&w photos and film credits.

The Masque of the Red Death and Other Tales of Horror. By Edgar Allan Poe, Ray Bradbury, et. al. Edited by Michael Sissons. London: A Panther Book, October 1964. No. 1755.
   Back cover has red-tinted photo of Vincent Price and Jane Asher from the Anglo-Amalgamated production; front cover is artwork of face resembling Price.

The Master Key. By John Fleming Wilson. New York: Grosset & Dunlap, c. 1915.
   Thirty-one pictures from the 1914 Universal serial; all save frontispiece are on unusual two-sided plates.

The Master Mind. By Marvin Dana, from the play by Daniel D. Carter. New York: Grosset & Dunlap, c. 1913.

Five photos from the stage production, including one double-page spread.

The Master Mystery. By Arthur B. Reeve and John W. Grey. From Scenarios by Arthur B. Reeve in Collaboration with John W. Grey and C. A. Logue. New York: Grosset & Dunlap, 1919.

Title page: "Profusely illustrated with photographic reproductions taken from the Houdini super-serial of the same name. A B. A. Rolfe production." Fifteen photos on double-sided plates from the 1919 Houdini serial. (Note: Petaja says "11 pictures" in *Photoplay Edition*; Miller says "13 stills" in *Photoplay Editions*.) Two photos, opposite pages 66 and 258, show the "Iron Terror" Automaton. (This copy has some pages [91–106] printed off-center; but no text is lost.) Reeve and Grey also collaborated on the Houdini film *Terror Island.*

Master of the World. Dell comic No. 1157. New York, N.Y.: Dell Publishing Co., Inc., 1961.

Tie-in comic to the 1961 American-International film with Vincent Price. No photos, only artwork. Inside front cover gives movie credits.

Master of the World see *Jules Verne's Master of the World*

The Merry Men and Other Tales and Fables: Strange Case of Dr. Jekyll and Mr. Hyde. By Robert Louis Stevenson. New York: Charles Scribner's Sons, 1917.

Contains one double-exposure photo of Richard Mansfield as both Jekyll and Hyde. (Mansfield was the first actor to play the role onstage.)

A Message From Mars: A Story. By Lester Lurgan. "Founded on the Popular Play of the Same Name by Richard Ganthony." London: Greening & Co., n.d.

"With 11 illustrations in half-tone, taken from the [1913 United Kingdom Films] cinematograph version of the play." Typographical error under first photo facing page 160: "'Do go away!' he cried, pe[t]ulantly."

Metropolis. By Thea von Harbou. London: Hutchinson & Co., n.d.

Four photos from the 1926 Fritz Lang film, "distributed by Wardour Films Co.," with Brigitte Helm; one shows the robot in metallic form.

"Midnight Phantom." In: *Boy's Cinema,* No. 871 (August 22, 1936), 13–20, 26.

"The police chief refuses his consent to his daughter's engagement to one of his lieutenants because the latter's brother had a criminal record. The chief is mysteriously murdered, and a famous criminologist declares the lieutenant to be the killer. A thrilling crime story, starring Reginald Denny and Lloyd Hughes." Four photos from the Reliable Pictures Corp. film, released in England by the Butcher's Film Service; credits on page 26.

The Million Dollar Mystery. By Harold MacGrath. Novelized from the scenario of F. Lonegan. New York: Grosset & Dunlap, c. 1915.
Fifty-eight stills from the 1914 Thanhouser Film Corp. serial with James Cruze.

"The Million Dollar Mystery." In: *Boy's Cinema*, No. 454 (August 25, 1928), 10–16.
"An enthralling story of a duel between the Secret Service and a ruthless gang of wrongdoers, starring James Kirkwood and Lila Lee." Two photos from the First National Pathé Films production. Page 2 contains a brief article, with cast list, about the film, noting: "Physical and moral courage and a gift for unraveling intrigue are not the only qualities essential to the successful Secret Service man. Above all things, he has to be clever in an all-round sense, and this cleverness must involve the ability to invest himself with personalities not his own; also complete mastery of the art of disguise."

The Miracle Man. By Frank L. Packard. New York: Grosset & Dunlap, c. 1914.
Four photos from the 1919 Lon Chaney movie, "Presented by Mayflower Photoplay Corporation."

The Miracle Man. By Frank L. Packard. New York and Chicago: A. L. Burt Company, c. 1914.
Dust jacket (only) has cover photo of Chester Morris, Sylvia Sidney, Irving Pichel (?), and John Wray as "The Frog," from the 1932 Paramount movie. (Paramount billed Wray as "the new Lon Chaney" in this film, rather than Boris Karloff, who also appeared in it.)

"The Miracle Man." In: *Boy's Cinema*, No. 141 (October 15, 1932), 1–8, 27.
"John Maddison, head of a gang of grafters, tries to exploit an old faith-healer known as the Patriarch; but the faith-healer wields such a mysterious power over them that the crooks are confounded. Starring Chester Morris, Sylvia Sidney, and Hobart Bosworth." Nine photos from the Paramount remake with Chester Morris as Maddison; John Wray plays the

Lon Chaney role of The Frog. Boris Karloff and Virginia Bruce are also in the cast list on page 26; Karloff appears in the photo on page 3.

Miss Pinkerton. By Mary Roberts Rinehart. New York: Grosset & Dunlap, c. 1932.
    Dust jacket (only) has one photo from the 1932 Warner Bros. movie with Joan Blondell.

Mr. & Mrs. North. Adapted from *The Norths Meet Murder.* By Frances & Richard Lockridge. New York: Grosset & Dunlap, c. 1940; Fifth printing, June 17, 1941.
    "An M-G-M Production starring Gracie Allen." Dust jacket (only) has one front-cover blue-tinted photo of Gracie Allen and William Post, Jr., from the 1941 movie.

"Mr. and Mrs. North." In: *Movie Story Magazine*, Vol. 17, No. 94 (February 1942), 38–41, 59–63.
    Four photos from the Loew's film with Gracie Allen and William Post, Jr. (The same issue has "The Wolf Man.")

"Mr. Moto's Gamble." Fictionized by Ann Silver. In: *Screen Romances*, 17, 109 (June 1938), 30–33, 110.
    Five photos from the 1938 20th Century–Fox film with Peter Lorre, Keye Luke, and Harold Huber. Lorre appears in two photos on page 32. This script was originally planned as a Charlie Chan film, but was converted to a Mr. Moto story when Warner Oland died.

"Mr. Moto's Last Warning." Fictionized by Helen McCoy [*sic* for McCloy]. In: *Screen Romances*, Vol. 18, No. 114 (November 1938), 72–75, 109–110.
    Six photos from the 20th Century–Fox film with Peter Lorre, Ricardo Cortez, John Carradine, and George Sanders.

Mr. Wu. By Louise Jordan Miln. New York: A. L. Burt, c. 1918.
    Four photos from the 1927 MGM movie with Lon Chaney. Color-photocopy of dust jacket has an additional photo scene with Chaney.

The Mocking Bird: An Underworld Story of the London Limehouse District. By Tod Browning. New York: Jacobsen-Hodgkinson Corporation, 1925. Paperback.
    Cover photo of Lon Chaney from the 1926 MGM film *The Blackbird*; three photos bound in, including one of Tod Browning. Back cover has six photos of Chaney's "Thousand Faces" from *The Monster, The Unholy Three,*

The Tower of Lies, Phantom of the Opera, Hunchback of Notre Dame, and *He Who Gets Slapped.*

Modern Mystery and Adventure Novels. Revised. Edited and abridged by Jay
   E. Greene. New York: Globe Book Company, c. 1951.
   Textbook with abridged versions of four novels, each illustrated with
scenes from its respective movie: *Portrait of Jennie* by Robert Nathan (Jennifer Jones, Joseph Cotton photos); *Jamaica Inn* by Daphne du Maurier
(Robert Newton, Maureen O'Sullivan photos); *The Thirty-Nine Steps* by
John Buchan (Robert Donat photos); *Dr. Jekyll and Mr. Hyde* by Robert
Louis Stevenson (Spencer Tracy photos). Frontispiece is composite of six
photos from all four movies. Library binding has additional photo of
Spencer Tracy as Jekyll.

Moon Zero Two. From the story for the film by Gavin Lyall, Frank Hardman, and Martin Davidson. Adapted by John Burke. New York: A Signet
   Book from New American Library, 1969. No. P4165.
   Front and back cover have reddish and white photos from the 1969 Hammer Film.

The Moonstone. By Wilkie Collins. London: The Literary Press Ltd., n.d.
   Dust jacket (only) has colored artwork showing Hindu Yandoo, played by
John Davidson, looking at frightened woman (Phyllis Barry in the role of
Ann Verinder) from the 1934 Monogram picture with David Manners. The
spine of jacket has and additional caricatured painting of Hindu not recognizable as Davidson. The front of jacket says "The Story of the Pathé Film."

"The Most Dangerous Game." Fictionized by Susan Conrad. In: *Screen
   Romances*, Vol. 28, No. 194 (July 1945), 51–53, 78–82.
   Five photos from the 1945 RKO version with John Loder, Edgar Barrier, and Noble Johnson. (Johnson had also appeared in the 1932 RKO
version with Joel McRea and Leslie Banks.)

Motion Picture Classic— 'The Lost World."

The Motion Picture Magazine— 'The Hunchback of Notre Dame" (Chaney).

Movie Action Magazine— 'The Walking Dead."

Movie Mirror— 'The Ghost Breakers."

Movie Story Magazine— "Abbott & Costello Meet Frankenstein," "Arsene
   Lupin Returns," "Arsenic and Old Lace," "The Black Cat" (Rathbone,

Lugosi), "The Beast with Five Fingers," "Black Friday," "The Blue Dahlia," "The Cat People," "Curse of the Cat People," "Dressed to Kill," "Dr. Cyclops," "Dr. Jekyll and Mr. Hyde" (Tracy), "The Falcon in Mexico," "The Falcon's Alibi," "Farewell, My Lovely," "Frankenstein Meets the Wolf Man," "Gaslight," "The Gay Falcon," "The Ghost Breakers," "The Ghost Catchers," "The Ghost of Frankenstein," "The Ghost Steps Out" ("The Time of Their Lives"), "The Gorilla" (Ritz Bros.), "The Gracie Allen Murder Case," "Hold That Ghost," "The House of Dracula," "The Hunchback of Notre Dame" (Laughton), "I Walked with a Zombie," "King Solomon's Mines," "Lady of Burlesque," "The Leopard Man," "The Lodger," "The Mad Ghoul," "Mr. and Mrs. North," "The Mummy's Ghost," "Nancy Drew, Reporter," "One Dangerous Night," "Over My Dead Body," "Raffles," "Song of the Thin Man," "The Spider," "The Spider Woman Strikes Back," "Tower of London," "The Uninvited," "Weird Woman," "Whispering Ghosts," "Whistling in Dixie," "Whistling in the Dark," "Who Done It?," and "The Wolf Man."

Moving Picture Stories— "The Bishop Murder Case," "A Blind Bargain" (Chaney), "The Gorilla" (1927), "Murder on the Roof," "Outside the Law" (Chaney), "Quits" (Chaney), "Steady Company" (Chaney), "Terror Island" (Houdini), and "The Violin Maker" (Chaney).

"The Mummy." Film Drama by Nina Wilcox Putnam and Richard Schayer. Story by James Whitlach. In *The Mystery Magazine* [cover: just *Mystery*], Vol. 7, No. 1 (January 1933), 19–23, 100–105.
  "Can the dead come to life? A story of the weird magic of old Egypt! A three-thousand-year-old mummy is brought into modern civilization with all of the sensations of a new age! Read the thrilling story here—then see the Universal Pictures mystery drama in your favorite theater." Story version in five chapters illustrated with eight photos from the 1932 film with Boris Karloff, Zita Johann, Edward Van Sloan, David Manners, and Noble Johnson. Eight photos appear, of all of these actors, including a scene of Johann during a Roman past life, not in the film as released.

"The Mummy." [Anon. author] Based on the story by Nina Wilcox Putnam and Richard Schayer. In: *Screen Romances*, Vol. 8, No. 45 (February 1933), 84–90, 111–12.
  Short story version, different from above (*Mystery Magazine*), illustrated with nine photos from the Universal film with Karloff, Zita Johann, Edward Van Sloan, and David Manners. One photo in common with *Mystery Magazine* version; others all different. Film credits given on page 84.

"The Mummy." [Anon. author] In: *The Film Star Weekly*, Vol. 1, No. 25 (May 13, 1933), 12, 17–18, 20–21, 23.
"An amazing drama of a love that was born again after centuries had passed." Another British fictionized version, with three photos from the Universal film with Boris Karloff.

"The Mummy." [Anon. author] In: *Boy's Cinema Annual 1934*, 71–80. Issued from The Fleetway House, Farringdon Street, London E.C.4.
"The Thing that came to life! Could it be true that a spell had raised a man from the dead, to bridge the gap of thirty-seven centuries? A gripping tale that links the modern World with mysterious Ancient Egypt, starring Boris Karloff, David Manners, and Zita Johann." Yet another fictionized version, with ten photos from the Universal film.

The Mummy. By Carl Dreadstone. Adapted from the screenplay by John L. Balderston. With an introduction by Ramsey Campbell. New York: Berkley Publishing Corporation, 1977.
Numerous photos from the 1932 Universal movie.

"The Mummy's Ghost." In: *Movie Story Magazine*, Vol. 17, No. 124 (August 1944), 52–53, 108–114.
One photo from the 1944 Universal film with Lon Chaney, John Carradine, and Ramsay Ames. Page 110 is a one-column insert story, "Chaney, Jr. Carries On," with photos of Chaney as the Man-Made Monster, the Wolf Man, the Frankenstein monster, the Mummy (from The Mummy's Ghost), and without makeup. This article refers to his third appearance as the Wolf Man in "The Devil's Brood"—a pre-release title of "The House of Frankenstein." (The same issue has "The Falcon in Mexico.")

"Murder at the Vanities." Fictionized by Faith Fenwick. In: *Screen Romances*, Vol. 10, No. 60 (May 1934), 67–73.
Twelve photos from the 1934 Paramount Picture with Jack Oakie, Kitty Carlisle, and Charles Middleton. After a six-page story which does not reveal the murderer's identity, page 73 is an announcement of a contest, with the result to be given in the July 1934 issue.

Murder by Decree. Adapted by Robert Weverka from the screenplay by John Hopkins. New York: Ballantine Books, 1979. No. 28062.
Cover has color artwork from the 1979 Avco Embassy release with Christopher Plummer as Holmes and James Mason as Watson. Separate photo section has seventeen b&w photos.

Murder, My Sweet see *Farewell, My Lovely*

"Murder on a Bridle Path." In: *Boy's Cinema*, No. 876 (September 26, 1936), 1–12, 25–27.

"When Violet Feverel is found dead in Central Park, apparently thrown and trampled by a horse, Detective-Inspector Piper decides that it must have been an accident. But Miss Hildegarde Withers convinces him that it was murder, and the two investigate a complicated case in which there is yet another killing before the guilty person is discovered. A first-class mystery, starring James Gleason." Six photos from the RKO Radio Pictures film with Helen Broderick in her one appearance as Withers, replacing Edna May Oliver (who left RKO for MGM in 1935); Broderick was immediately succeeded by ZaSu Pitts in the next two films.

"Murder on a Honeymoon." In: *Boy's Cinema*, No. 815 (July 27, 1935), 11–20, 25–28.

"In a seaplane flying from Los Angeles to Catalina Island one of the passengers is murdered; and Miss Hildegarde Withers, a middle-aged school teacher, wires from Avalon to New York for Detective-Inspector Piper—who finds himself up against one of the toughest problems of his career." Five photos from the 1935 Radio Pictures film with Edna May Oliver and James Gleason. Credits on page 2. (The same issue has "A Shot in the Dark.")

Murder on the Roof: Photoplay Title of The Broadway Murders: A Night Club Mystery. By Edward J. Doherty. New York: Grosset & Dunlap, c. 1929.

Tie-in with the 1930 Columbia film, but no photos on dust jacket or internally; jacket has artwork drawing of three chorus girls. Title page lists *Murder on the Roof* in larger letters above *The Broadway Murders*; jacket reverses the order and emphasis.

"Murder on the Roof." By Helen Hoyt. In: *Moving Picture Stories*, Vol. 36, No. 842 (March 4, 1930), 18–19, 24 (part 1); Vol. 36, No. 843 (March 18, 1930), 16–17, 25 (part 2).

Part 1 has two photos, Part 2 has one photo from the 1930 Columbia mystery with Dorothy Revier and Raymond Hatton. (The No. 842 issue also has part 2 of "The Bishop Murder Case.")

"Murders in the Rue Morgue." Fictionized by Watkins E. Wright. In: *Screen Romances*, Vol. 6, No. 34 (March 1932), 40–46, 100.

Six photos from the 1932 Universal picture with Bela Lugosi, Sidney Fox, and Noble Johnson.

The Murders in the Rue Morgue and Other Tales of Horror. By Edgar Allan
Poe. New York: Grosset & Dunlap, n.d.
   Both endpapers plus seven internal photos are from Universal's 1932 film
with Bela Lugosi. Color dust jacket shows artwork of green ape hovering
over unconscious woman with bright red hair, stretched horizontally on
bed (similar to photograph, opposite page 228, of ape over actress Betsy
Ross Clarke). Back cover of dust jacket has advertising blurbs for four Grosset & Dunlap photoplay novels, *Frankenstein, Murders in the Rue Morgue,
Dr. Jekyll and Mr. Hyde,* and *Dracula*; each illustrated with a b&w photo
from the respective film. (These particular photos, however, do not appear
in the various photoplay editions themselves.)

Mysterious Dr. Fu Manchu see *Insidious Dr. Fu Manchu*

The Mysterious Island. By Jules Verne. New York: Grosset & Dunlap, n.d.
   Eight single-page photos and one double-page photo plus endpaper photos from the 1929 MGM movie with Lionel Barrymore.

Mysterious Island. Dell Movie Classic comic No. 1213. New York: Dell Publishing Co., Inc., 1961.
   Comic book version of the 1961 Columbia film with special effects by
Ray Harryhausen. Front cover has two color photos from the film, back
cover has three monotone photos. Inside front cover has five b&w photos.

Mysterious Island. By Jules Verne. New York: Permabooks, published by
Pocket Books, Inc., 1962. No. M 6002.
   Front cover has drawing and two color photos from the Columbia film with
special effects by Ray Harryhausen; back cover has artwork of submarine.

"Mysterious Island." Adapted by George Scullin. In: *Screen Stories,* Vol. 61,
No. 1 (January 1962), 33–37, 64–67.
   Eleven photos from Ray Harryhausen Columbia film with Michael
Craig, Joan Greenwood, and Herbert Lom.

Mystery Magazine— "The Mummy."

The Mystery Mind. By Arthur B. Reeve and John W. Grey; novelization
by Marc Edmund Jones. New York: Grosset & Dunlap, c. 1920.
   Four photos from the 1920 serial, "Produced by Supreme Pictures, Inc.
and released by Pioneer Film Corporation."

Mystery of Edwin Drood. By Charles Dickens. "The completion of this novel
is by Ruth Alexander following the ending adopted by Universal Pictures." London: The Queensway Press, n.d. [1935].

Five photos from the 1935 Universal film with Claude Rains, Valerie Hobson, and David Manners. Manners appears in photos opposite pages 32 and 80; Rains appears opposite page 272; Hobson, opposite 80 and 304.

"The Mystery of Edwin Drood." Fictionized by Mary Chadbourne Brown. In: *Screen Romances*, Vol. 12, No. 70 (March 1935), 48–52, 99. Five photos from the Universal film with David Manners, Claude Rains, and Valerie Hobson.

"The Mystery of Edwin Drood." In: *Boy's Cinema*, No. 822 (September 14, 1935), 9–14, 25–26. "The story of a man with a dual character, who is torn between affection and jealousy, who loves his nephew, but is feared and disliked by his nephew's fiancée, which leads to a strange and mysterious crime." Six photos from the Universal film with David Manners, Claude Rains, and Valerie Hobson. Credits on page 26.

The Mystery of the Hope Diamond. By H. L. Gates. Together with the Romantic Personal Narrative of May Yohe (Lady Francis Hope). Title page reads: "as set down by H. L. Gates … from the Personal Narrative of Lady Francis Hope (May Yohe)." New York: International Copyright Bureau, 1921. Paperback. Twelve photos from the 1921 Kosmik Films fifteen-chapter serial featuring Boris Karloff in dual role, one of which is that of turbaned priest. Grace Darmond is the heroine and Harry Carter the villain. The back cover provides a roster of twenty-five owners of the Hope diamond and their unhappy fates.

The Mystery of the Louvre. By Arthur Bernède. Illustrated with Scenes from the Photo-Play. A Universal Production Starring Elmir Vautier And René Navarre. The Crime Series. London: The Readers Library Publishing Company Ltd., n.d. Copyright edition No. 268. Eight black and white photos (printed on four double sided plates) from "A European Picture." Dust jacket has color artwork on front and back. Front panel shows wraithlike ghost, next to green statue, threatening man holding a gun; margin area is b&w illustration of ship's rope ladder along right side, with bottom panel showing b&w illustration of blackjack, bullets, gun, knife, brass knuckles, etc. Devilish b&w face in lower right corner has "Crime Series" imprinted on it. Back panel is color illustration of ghastly green hand clutching for packet of letters on table next to sleeping, bobbed-hair brunette. Left and lower margins show b&w illustrations of saw, file, drill, poison, ink, acid bottles, cards, Bank of England notes, jewelry, etc. Chapter 1 of the novel dates the story to 1925. (Note: The same author's follow-up novel, *The Haunted House: Further Adventures of Chantecoq The Famous Detective* [London: Readers Library, n.d.; No. 299] is not connected in any way to the 1928 film of the same title by Benjamin Christensen.)

Mystery of the Wax Museum. Edited with an introduction by Richard
    Koszarski. Wisconsin/Warner Bros. Screenplay series. Madison, Wisc.
    : University of Wisconsin Press, 1979.
    Film script of the 1933 Warner Bros. film with Lionel Atwill, Fay Wray,
and Glenda Farrell; illustrated with twenty-two internal photos, and one
more on the dust jacket.

Mystery of the Yellow Room. By Gaston Leroux. New York: Grosset & Dun-
    lap, c. 1908.
    Four photos from the 1919 Realart Pictures Corporation movie; also
another yellow-tinted photo on dust jacket cover (same photo on front and
back covers).

"Nancy Drew, Reporter." In: *Moving Picture Stories*, Vol. 12, No. 60 (April
    1939), 38, 40, 75–78.
    Three photos from the Warner Bros. picture with Bonita Granville as
Nancy Drew. A fourth picture appears in the table of contents listing on
page 4.

Nathaniel Hawthorne's Twice Told Tales. Dell Movie Classic comic No.
    12–840–401. New York: Dell Publishing Co., Inc., 1963.
    Comic book version. Front cover has color photo from the 1963 Admi-
ral Pictures/United Artists film; inside front cover has three b&w photos
and film credits. Inside back cover has b&w artwork montage of scenes from
the film.

"Nick Carter—Master Detective." In: *Boy's Cinema*, No. 1063 (April 27,
    1940), 1–6.
    "An exciting adventure of a famous American Detective, and how he
unraveled the mystery of the vanished blue-prints. Starring Walter Pidgeon." Seven photos from the MGM film. Also in the cast are Henry Hull,
Donald Meek, and Martin Kosleck.

"The Night Club Lady." In: *Film Star Weekly*, Vol. 1, No. 12 (February 11,
    1933), 12, 17–19, 23.
    Three photos from the Columbia Pictures film with Adolphe Menjou
as Thatcher Colt.

The Night Club Lady: Photoplay Title of About the Murder of the Night Club Lady see *About the Murder of the Night Club Lady*

"Night Must Fall." Fictionized by Eileen Chapman. In: *Screen Romances*, Vol. 17, No. 98 (July 1937), 38–41, 104, 106–108.
Seven photos from the MGM adaptation of Emlyn Williams's play, with Robert Montgomery, Rosalind Russell, and Dame May Whitty. (The same issue has "The 13th Chair," also with Dame May Whitty.)

Night of the Living Dead. By John Russo. New York: Warner Paperback Library, 1974. No. 76–410.
Sixteen pages of b&w photos from the George Romero movie bound in.

The Night Stalker. By Jeff Rice, screenplay adapted by Richard Matheson. New York: Pocket Books, December 1973. No. 78343.
Front cover has color photo of Darrin McGavin from the 1972 ABC made-for-TV film.

The Norths Meet Murder see *Mr. & Mrs. North*

Nosferatu: The Vampire. A novel by Paul Monette based on Werner Herzog's screenplay. New York: Avon Books, 1979. No. 44107.
Eight glossy pages bound in with twelve b&w photos; front cover has color artwork from the 20th Century–Fox film with Klaus Kinski; back cover has three color photos.

The Oblong Box see *Fantastic Tales*

Odor of Violets see *Eyes in the Night*

"Of Mice and Men." Fictionized by Robert Arthur. In: *Screen Romances*, Vol. 18, No. 130 (March 1940), 19–23, 64, 66–67.
Included here for its Lon Chaney, Jr., connection. Nine photos from the 1940 United Artists film, with Burgess Meredith, Charles Bickford, and Chaney. Four pictures show Chaney; an additional fifth, "between the scenes" photo of Chaney, Meredith, and Bickford appears on page 78.

The Old Dark House. By J. B. Priestley. New York: Grosset & Dunlap, c. 1928.
Four photos from Universal's 1932 film with Boris Karloff. (Karloff is in all four.)

Oliver Twist. By Charles Dickens. New York: The Charles Renard Company, Publishers, 1925.

Twenty b&w photos ("Life Portraits") on ten double-sided plates from Sol Lesser's 1922 Principal Pictures Corporation film version, with Jackie Coogan as Oliver. Lon Chaney appears as Fagin, opposite pages 53 and 148.

"One Dangerous Night." In: *Movie Story Magazine*, Vol. 14, No. 105 (January 1943), 66, 68, 70–72.
Three photos from the 1943 Columbia mystery with Warren William as the Lone Wolf, and Eric Blore. (The same issue has "The Cat People" and "I Married a Witch.")

"One Is Guilty." Fictionized by Cass Calhoun. In: *Screen Romances*, Vol. 10, No. 60 (May 1934), 44–48, 111–113.
Eight photos from the 1934 Columbia Pictures mystery with Ralph Bellamy, Shirley Grey, and J. Carroll Naish.

Orgy of the Dead. By Edward D. Wood, Jr. Special Introduction by Forrest J Ackerman. San Diego, California: Greenleaf Classics, Inc., 1966. No. GC205.
Color artwork cover; sixty-one interior b&w photos from the 1966 Astra Productions movie with Criswell. Some photos are "behind the scenes" shots, e.g., of Ed Wood (p. 107).

Original Adventures of Sherlock Holmes. By A. Conan Doyle. New York: R. F. Fenno & Company, n.d. (Handwritten inscription dated 1910.)
Ten photos from the stage production with William Gillette as Holmes; these photos show actors in costume but not within stage sets. Front cover shows dye-ink drawing of Gillette as Holmes; compare photo at page 163. (Same ten photos appear in *Sherlock Holmes* [see entry], to which this volume is very similar; but these copies are dissimilar to *Tales of Sherlock Holmes*, with different Gillette photos.)

Outside the Law. Based on the Motion Picture Story by Tod Browning. New York: Jacobsen-Hodgkinson Corporation, c. 1926. Paperback.
Three internal photos from the 1921 Universal film with Lon Chaney; two more photos on front and back covers. Pictures include Chaney in two roles, "Black Mike Silva" and Oriental "Joe Wang."

"Outside the Law." Adapted from the Screen Play by Beulah Poynter. In: *Moving Picture Stories*, Vol. 28, No. 705 (June 29, 1926), 12–15, 31.
Three photos from the silent Universal film, one showing Lon Chaney in Oriental makeup.

"Over My Dead Body." In: *Movie Story Magazine*, Vol. 14, 106 (February 1943), 50–51, 107–110.
Three photos from 20th Century–Fox mystery-comedy with Milton Berle.

"The Penguin Pool Mystery." In: *The Film Star Weekly*, Vol. 2, No. 35 (July 22, 1933), 27.
One-page plot summary with three photos from the RKO Radio Pictures film with Edna May Oliver, James Gleason, and Robert Armstrong.

The People That Time Forgot. By Edgar Rice Burroughs. New York: Ace Books, c. 1918 [1977]. No. 65946-2.
Sixteen page insert of b&w photos from the 1977 American-International movie with Patrick Wayne and Doug McClure.

Perils of Pauline. By Charles Goddard. New York: Hearst's International Library Co., c. 1914 by The Star Co., c. 1915 by Hearst's International Library Co., Inc.
Fifteen photos from the 1914 Pathé serial with Pearl White.

"The Perils of Pauline." In: *Boy's Cinema*, No. 738 (February 3, 1934), 2–6, 26–27.
"A secret formula that spelled destruction for entire nations if it found its way into the wrong hands. This was the subject of the strange and perilous quest undertaken by Professor Hargrave and his beautiful daughter. A powerful serial of Romance and Adventure in distant lands." "Episode 1" illustrated with seven photos from the Universal serial starring Evalyn Knapp and Robert Allen. (The same issue has "The Kennel Murder Case.")

"The Perils of Pauline." Fictionized by Marjorie Bailey. In: *Screen Romances*, Vol. 28, No. 218 (July 1947), 37–39, 64–68.
Five photos from the 1947 Paramount film with Betty Hutton.

The Phantom Cracksman see *Cleek of Scotland Yard*

The Phantom of the Opera. By Gaston Leroux. Translated by Alexander Teixeira de Mattos. London: Hutchinson & Co., n.d.
Eight internal photos from the 1925 Universal film with Lon Chaney. Frontispiece shows Chaney in Red Death costume; photos opposite pages 148 and 172 show good views of Phantom make-up. Photo opposite page 204 appears on dust jacket of the American version by Grosset & Dunlap. Title page says, "Illustrated With Scenes From The Photoplay."

The Phantom of the Opera. By Gaston Leroux. Translated by Alexander Teixeira de Mattos. London: The Readers Library, n.d. [No. 104].

No internal photos. Dust jacket has two colored photos from the 1925
Universal film with Lon Chaney: front, Christine and Raoul hold each
other at the foot of a stair, with the Phantom as the Red Death at the stair
top; back, the unmasked Phantom, in profile, and Christine lean over the
cabinet with the scorpion and grasshopper. Front jacket cover has note,
"Film Edition," with partially removed sticker reading "Author [of] The
Mys[tery] Of [The Yellow Room]."

The Phantom of the Opera. By Gaston Leroux. Translated by Alexander
Teixeira de Mattos. London: The Readers Library, n.d. (Reprint of No.
104, with photos).

British edition with eight photos, bound in on four double-sided plates,
from the 1930 re-release of the Universal film. Title page says, "Illustrated
with Scenes from the Talking, Singing, Orchestrated and Colour Picture
starring Lon Chaney and Mary Philbin."

The Phantom of the Opera. By Gaston Leroux. New York: Grosset & Dunlap, c. 1911.

Four photos from Universal's 1925 Lon Chaney movie, plus two colored
drawings, plus additional hand-colored movie photo of grand staircase scene
at masked ball, wrapping around the entire dust jacket. Only the frontispiece shows Chaney, from a distance, in Phantom make-up. Title page
says, "Illustrated By André Castaigne And With Scenes From The Universal Production Starring Lon Chaney."

"Phantom of the Opera." Fictionized by Nancy Webb. In: *Screen Romances*,
Vol. 28, No. 172 (September 1943), 46–49, 62, 64, 66.

Full page, full color photo of Susanna Foster and Nelson Eddy on page
46; seven additional b&w photos from 1943 Universal film with Claude
Rains as the Phantom. Credits on page 48.

The Phantom of the Opera. By Gaston Leroux. New York: Popular Library,
October 1962. No. PC1020.

Front cover has color photo of Herbert Lom and Heather Sears from the
Hammer/Universal-International film.

"The Phantom of the Opera." Adapted by George Scullin. In: *Screen Stories*, Vol. 61, No. 10 (October 1962), 34–37, 50–51, 54.

Five photos from the 1962 Hammer film with Herbert Lom. Additional
sixth photo appears in "behind the scenes article" on pages 47–48. (The
same issue contains "The Wonderful World of the Brothers Grimm.")

The Phantom Planet. Dell Movie Classic comic No. 1234. New York: Dell
 Publishing Co., Inc., 1961.
   Front cover has color artwork of floating astronaut, and color photo of
creature. Inside front cover has five b&w photos and credits from the Four
Crown Productions Inc. film.

Philo Vance Murder Cases. By S. S. Van Dine. New York and London: Charles
 Scribner's Sons, 1936.
   An omnibus volume with three Philo Vance mysteries, *The Scarab Murder Case, The Kennel Murder Case* and *The Dragon Murder Case.* Included
are photos of four film actors in the role of Vance: William Powell, Paul
Lukas, Warren William, and Basil Rathbone. Artwork portraits of Vance,
and of author Van Dine, also appear. The volume has an introduction by
the author, a biography of Van Dine by William Stanley Braithwaite, a
"biography" of Vance by Y. B. Garden, and Van Dine's "Twenty Rules for
Writing Detective Stories." The dust jacket shows three overlapping file
cards, connected with the stories; it has no photo or artwork elements from
the films, but does mention the "motion picture stars" whose photographs
are included in the book.

Photoplay Studies—Things to Come see *Things to Come*

The Picture of Dorian Gray. By Oscar Wilde. Cleveland and New York: The
 World Publishing Company, Inc., Tower Books edition third printing,
 March 1945.
   Dust jacket has six photos from the 1945 MGM movie with Hurd
Hatfield. (This particular copy has three extra photos of Hatfield pasted in
on blank leaves, one in color and with the handwritten inscription, "Love,
Hurd.")

The Picture of Dorian Gray. Story Adaptation of Screen Play by C. P. Chad-
 sey. New York: Caxton House, Inc., c. 1945.
   Cover says "Film Books"; title page says "Motion Picture Books." This
is a 48–page booklet telling the story of the film with 37 stills (one split
over two pages) and a color artwork cover of scenes from the MGM film
with Hurd Hatfield, George Sanders, Donna Reed, and Angela Lansbury.

"The Picture of Dorian Gray." Fictionized by Frances Lord. In: *Screen
 Romances,* Vol. 28, No. 192 (May 1945), 46–47, 80–85.
   Five photos from the 1945 MGM film with Hurd Hatfield, George
Sanders, Donna Reed, and Angela Lansbury.

Picture Show—"Devil Girl From Mars" and "Laugh, Clown, Laugh" (Chaney).

Pit and the Pendulum. Adapted by Lee Sheridan from the Richard Matheson screenplay. New York: Lancer Books, c. 1961. No. 71–303.
Front and back covers have four photos from the American-International movie; also a poster drawing on the first page inside the front cover.

Poe's Tales of Terror. Adapted by Eunice Sudak from the screenplay by Richard Matheson. New York: Lancer Books, c. 1962. No. 71–325.
Front and back covers have four photos from the 1962 American-International movie.

Portrait of Jennie see *Modern Mystery and Adventure Novels*

"Postal Inspector." In: *Boy's Cinema,* No. 885 (November 28, 1936), 11–18, 26–27.
"A city in the path of disaster. Somewhere in that city, a gang of desperate mail-robbers seeking to escape with their loot, while a determined employee of the Government strives to track them down. A powerful drama of a Service that knows no barriers, starring Ricardo Cortez, Patricia Ellis, Bela Lugosi, and Michael Loring." Credits on page 27.

The Postman Always Rings Twice. By James M. Cain. New York: Grosset & Dunlap, c. 1934.
Dust jacket photo from the MGM film with Lana Turner and John Garfield.

Premature Burial. By Max Hallan Danne, based on the screenplay by Charles Beaumont and Ray Russell. New York: Lancer Books, c. 1962. No. 71–313.
Front and back covers have four photos from the American-International movie.

Prisoners. By Franz Molnar. New York: Grosset & Dunlap, c. 1925.
Illustrated with seven internal photos, including endpapers, from First National Picture with Bela Lugosi in a pre–Dracula role. Dust jacket has four additional photos, including, on back cover, pictures of "Corinne Griffith and Ian Keith" and "Corinne Griffith and Bela Lugosi." Lugosi appears twice in the internal photos, facing page 98 and on back endpaper.

Psycho. By Robert Bloch. Greenwich, Conn.: Crest Book/Fawcett Publications, Inc., c. 1959, second Crest printing, August 1960. No. s385.

Front and back covers have photos of Janet Leigh from the Paramount movie directed by Alfred Hitchcock.

The Public Defender: Photoplay Title of The Splendid Crime. By George Goodchild. New York: Grosset & Dunlap, n.d.
Four photos from the 1931 RKO movie starring Richard Dix; dust jacket has color drawing of Dix and two others from the film. Photo facing page 88 shows Boris Karloff in a minor role.

Queen Kong. By James Moffat. London: Everest Books Ltd.
Paperback with color photo cover of Queen Kong from the Dexter Films Ltd. Production; eleven internal b&w photos bound in a separate section.

Queen of Blood. By Charles Nuetzel. Special Introduction by Forrest J Ackerman. San Diego, Calif.: Greenleaf Classics, Inc., 1966. No. GC206.
Color artwork cover; thirty interior b&w photos from the 1966 American-International film with Basil Rathbone, John Saxon, and Florence Marly as Velana.

Quincy Adams Sawyer. By Charles Felton Pidgin. Revised edition. New York: Grosset & Dunlap, c. 1900.
Eight photos from the 1922 "Metro—S. L Special Motion Picture Production," three showing Lon Chaney.

"Quits." By Richard Ellison. In: *Moving Picture Stories*, Vol. 6, No. 139 (August 27, 1915), 19–22.
Three photos from the 1915 Rex one-reel film showing Lon Chaney in the role of French George; additional photo of Jack J. Clark.

R.U.R. (Rossum's Universal Robots). By Karl Capek, translated by Paul Selver. Garden City, N.Y.: Doubleday, Page & Company, 1923.
Four photos from the Theatre Guild Stage production.

The Radio Detective. By Arthur B. Reeve. New York: Grosset & Dunlap, c. 1926.
Four photos from the 1926 serial. Dust jacket shows additional hand-colored photo, with note, "Illustrated with Scenes from the Photoplay / A Universal Production."

Raffles: The Amateur Cracksman. By E. W. Hornung. New York: A. L. Burt Company, c. 1899.

Four photos from the 1925 Universal Pictures film with House Peters as Raffles; dust jacket has additional colored photo on front cover.

"Raffles." By Leonard Van Noppen. Based on the story by E. W. Hornung. In: *Screen Book*, Vol. 5, No. 2 (August 1930), 18–54, 90, 92–106.
Thirty-three photos from the United Artists Production with Ronald Colman, Branwell [*sic*] Fletcher, and Kay Francis; credits on page 19. A thirty-fourth photo appears on page 4, behind the table of contents.

"Raffles." In: *Movie Story Magazine*, Vol. 14, No. 70 (February 1940), 22–25, 71–73.
Eight photos from the United Artists Picture with David Niven and Olivia De Havilland. Additional photo on table of contents, page 5; also full color cover of the magazine. (The same issue has "The Hunchback of Notre Dame.")

Raffles: Further Adventures of the Amateur Cracksman. By E. W. Hornung. New York: Grosset & Dunlap, c. 1901.
Four photos from the 1930 Samuel Goldwyn Production with Ronald Colman.

Rasputin and the Empress. Novelized by Val Lewton from the screenplay by Charles MacArthur. New York: Grosset & Dunlap, 1933.
Endpapers have fourteen photos from the 1932 MGM movie; dust jacket has color portrait of the three Barrymores (John, Lionel, Ethel) on front, plus five b&w photos on back.

"The Raven." Fictionized by G. H. Connaughton. In: *Romantic Movie Stories*, 11, 15 (June 1935), 12–16, 70–71.
"A Universal Picture starring Bela Lugosi and Karloff." Ten photos (including raven inset) from the 1935 production; film credits on page 13.

"The Raven." In: *Boy's Cinema*, No. 823 (September 21, 1935), 11–18.
"'The Raven' was the emblem of death! Doctor Vollin, thwarted by a girl, plans a fiendish and diabolical revenge, using a crook whom he has transformed into a monster for his fell purpose. A dramatic thriller, starring Boris Karloff and Bela Lugosi." Six photos from the Universal Pictures production.

The Raven. Adapted by Eunice Sudak from the Richard Matheson screenplay. New York: Lancer Books, 1963. No. 70–034.
Front cover has four photos, of Karloff, Lorre, Price, and Olive Sturgess from the American-International film; back cover has one photo of Sturgess.

The Raven. Dell Movie Classic comic No. 12–680–309. New York: Dell Publishing Co., Inc., 1963.

Front cover has color photos of Vincent Price, and Jack Nicholson with Olive Sturgess from the American-International film. Inside front cover is b&w photo montage of raven, Karloff, Price, Lorre, Sturgess, and iron maiden, with film credits.

The Red House. By George Agnew Chamberlain. New York: Grosset & Dunlap, 1945.

Dust jacket (only) has photo of Edward G. Robinson and Judith Anderson on front, Julie London on back, from the 1947 United Artists movie.

Reptilicus. By Dean Owen. Based on an original story by Sidney Pink. Screenplay by Ib Melchior. Derby, Connecticut: Monarch Books, Inc., 1961. No. MM605.

Front cover has reddish-tinted photo of monster from the American-International movie; back cover is silhouette photo of monster flying.

The Return of Chandu see *Chandu the Magician*

The Return of Dr. Fu Manchu. By Sax Rohmer. New York: A. L. Burt Company, c. 1916; 3rd printing, November 1918.

Four photos from the 1930 Paramount film with Warner Oland. (Two variant copies, also 3rd printing: One photo in each as frontispiece: same frontispiece on first; photo opposite page 232 used as frontispiece on second.)

"Return of The Terror." Fictionized by Lebbeus Mitchell. In: *Screen Romances*, Vol. 11, No. 63 (August 1934), 54–58, 107–109.

Five photos from the 1934 First National Picture with Mary Astor, Lyle Talbot, Frank McHugh, J. Carroll Naish, Frank Reicher, Irving Pichel, and Charles Grapewin. Credit block says, "Based on the Novel by Edgar Wallace." *Encyclopedia of Fantastic Film* and *Revenge of the Creature Features Movie Guide* both describe this film as a remake of the 1928 *The Terror.* The story here, however, is quite different from the photoplay novel; it is not a remake. (Table of contents reads "The Return," not "Return"; the same issue has "The Thin Man.")

The Revenge of Frankenstein. Based on a screenplay by Jimmy Sangster with additional dialogue by Hurford James. London: A Panther Book, 1958. No. 839.

Front cover has color drawing of monster suspended in glass case; back cover has red-tinted photo of monster from the Hammer film.

The Rise of the House of Rothschild. By Count Egon Caesar Corti. Translated from the German by Brian and Beatrix Lunn. New York: Grosset & Dunlap, c. 1928.

Endpapers (only) have 16 photos from the 1934 20th Century Pictures film *House of Rothschild* with George Arliss, Loretta Young, and Boris Karloff. Karloff appears in four of them (one with his back to the camera).

"The River House Mystery." In: *Boy's Cinema,* No. 835 (December 14, 1935), 13–19, 27.

"A tale of mystery with an unexpected ending, related by an ardent member of the Criminologist Club. Starring George Mulcaster and Ena Moon." Four photos from the Universal Pictures production. Credits on page 2.

The Road to Mandalay. By Tod Browning and Herman J. Mankiewicz. New York: Jacobsen-Hodgkinson Corporation, n.d. Paperback.

Front cover has color picture from the 1926 MGM film with Lon Chaney; back cover has six more photos; inside are thirteen more on three bound-in pages.

Robur the Conqueror see *Jules Verne's Master of the World*

"The Rogues' Tavern." In: *Boy's Cinema,* No. 868 (August 1, 1936), 13–18, 25–27.

"A detective and his sweetheart come by chance to a lonely tavern, and at once become involved in a series of strange crimes. Is the murderer a wolf or fiend in human shape? A strange mystery, starring Wallace Ford." Six photos from the Mercury Pictures film, also starring Marjorie Burns and Clara Kimball Young. Credits on page 27. (The same issue has the final chapter of *Flash Gordon,* Episode 13, "Rocketing to Earth.")

The Romance of Elaine. By Arthur B. Reeve. "With Frontispiece." Half-title page reads, "The Romance of Elaine / A Detective Novel / Sequel to the 'Exploits' / By Arthur B. Reeve." New York and London: Harper & Bros., c. 1916. Spine reads, "*Craig Kennedy Stories* / Arthur Reeve / *The Romance of Elaine* / Vol. 10."

Romance is a Pathé serial from 1915, but the frontispiece (only) photo of Pearl White, here, is a reprint of the illustration facing page 106 of *The Exploits of Elaine,* another Pathé serial from 1914.

Romantic Movie Stories—"After the Thin Man," "The Black Cat" (Karloff, Lugosi), "The Black Room," "The Raven," and "The Thin Man."

Rossum's Universal Robots see *R.U.R.*

"S.O.S. Coast Guard." In: *Boy's Cinema*, No. 1031 (September 16, 1939), Cover and 2–7.

"Vivid drama and high adventure surge through the pages of this pulsing serial story of the men who keep watch on the American seaboard." Four photos from the Republic Pictures serial "Episode 1: Disaster at Sea" with Ralph Byrd, Bela Lugosi, and Richard Alexander. (Lugosi is not pictured here.) This chapter ends with the teaser: "Why did Boroff send Thorg to sunder the moorings of the Carfax and send her to her doom? Are Terry Kent and Jean Norman destined to perish within the sinking cargo-steamer? Will Boroff succeed in evading justice? Will the terrible gas that the ruthless scoundrel has invented spread disaster and destruction through creation some day and secure world supremacy for Morvania? Don't miss 'Barrage of Death,' next week's gripping episode of this terrific serial."

Sardonicus and Other Stories. By Ray Russell. New York: Ballantine Books, 1961. No. 540.

Front cover has color drawing of Sardonicus removing mask; back cover has red-tinted photo from the William Castle movie from Columbia Pictures.

The Scarab Murder Case. By S. S. Van Dine. With a new introduction by Chris Steinbrunner. Boston, Mass.: Gregg Press, 1980.

Reprint of non-photoplay 1929 edition, with new inclusion of reproductions of promotional material (with photos) for the 1937 British Paramount film with Wilfred Hyde-White as Philo Vance.

The Scarab Murder Case see *Philo Vance Murder Cases*

The Scars of Dracula. By Angus Hall. New York: Beagle Books, First Printing, April 1971. No. 94071.

Front cover has color photo of Christopher Lee as Dracula, grasping knife in woman's prostrate body. Back cover gives film credits from the 1970 Hammer film.

Scream and Scream Again. By Peter Saxon. New York: Paperback Library, c. 1966, Second Printing, February 1970. No. 63–273.

Cover has two color photos from 1970 American-International picture with Vincent Price, Christopher Lee, and Peter Cushing (who do not appear in the cover photos). Hammer starlet Yutte Stensgaard appears in right-hand photo. Cover says "Soon to be an American International Motion Picture."

Screen Book Magazine—"The Hunchback of Notre Dame" (Laughton), "The Man Who Laughs," "Raffles," and "The Unholy Night."

Screen Romances— "After the Thin Man," "Arsene Lupin," "Bedlam," "The Big Sleep," "The Bride of Frankenstein," "Bulldog Drummond Escapes," "Bulldog Drummond Strikes Back," "Busman's Honeymoon," "The Case of the Curious Bride," "The Case of the Howling Dog," "Charlie Chan at Monte Carlo," "Charlie McCarthy, Detective," "The Crosby Case," "The Climax," "Devil's Island," "Dr. Jekyll and Mr. Hyde" (Tracy), "The Dragon Murder Case," "Ellery Queen's Penthouse Mystery," "Hold That Ghost," "The Hound of the Baskervilles," "The House of Rothschild," "The Hunchback of Notre Dame" (Laughton), "Invisible Agent," "The Invisible Woman," "The Kennel Murder Case," "The Lady Vanishes," "Mad Love," "The Maltese Falcon," "The Man Who Knew Too Much," "The Man Who Reclaimed His Head," "The Mandarin Mystery," "The Mark of the Vampire," "The Most Dangerous Game," "Mr. Moto's Gamble," "Mr. Moto's Last Warning," "The Mummy," "Murder at the Vanities," "Murders in the Rue Morgue," "The Mystery of Edwin Drood," "Night Must Fall," "Of Mice and Men," "One Is Guilty," "The Perils of Pauline" (Hutton), "Phantom of the Opera" (Rains), "The Picture of Dorian Gray," "Return of The Terror," "Secret of the Blue Room," "Sherlock Holmes," "Sherlock Holmes and the Secret Weapon," "Sherlock Holmes and the Voice of Terror," "The Spiral Staircase," "Tarzan," "Tarzan and His Mate," "Thank You, Mr. Moto," "The Thief of Bagdad" (Sabu), "The Thin Man," "The Thin Man Goes Home," "Think Fast, Mr. Moto," "The Thirteenth Chair," "Topper Returns," "The Uninvited," "Whistling in Brooklyn," "Who Done It?" and "You'll Find Out."

Screen Stories— "Fantastic Voyage," "The First Men in the Moon," "Forbidden Planet," "The Ghost and Mr. Chicken," "The Hunchback of Notre Dame" (Laughton), "The Innocents," "A Journey to the Center of the Earth," "The List of Adrian Messenger," "The Man Who Reclaimed His Head," "Mysterious Island," "The Phantom of the Opera" (Lom), "They Might Be Giants," "The Thirteenth Guest," "The Three Worlds of Gulliver," "20,000 Leagues Under the Sea," and "The Wonderful World of the Brothers Grimm."

The Second Floor Mystery: Photoplay Title of The Agony Column. By Earl Derr Biggers. New York: Grosset & Dunlap, c. 1916.
Four photos from the 1930 Warner Bros. movie with Richard Greene and Loretta Young. *The Agony Column* extends to page 194; a second story,

Fifty Candles, is bound after it, with a half-title page immediately after a copyright page, and text starting immediately, numbered pages 9—(159).

The Second Hammer Horror Film Omnibus. By John Burke. London: Pan Books Ltd., 1967. No. M223.
  Novelizations of four movies, with a colored picture or drawing of each on front and back covers: *The Reptile; Dracula—Prince of Darkness*; *Rasputin —The Mad Monk*; and *The Plague of the Zombies.*

Secret Beyond the Door. By Rufus King. New York: Triangle Books, 1947.
  Library binding has same photo on front and back covers from the 1948 Universal International movie with Joan Bennett and Michael Redgrave.

"Secret of the Blue Room." Fictionized by H. A. Keller. In: *Screen Romances,* Vol. 9, No. 53 (October 1933), 46–50, 111.
  Five photos from the 1933 Universal picture with Lionel Atwill, Paul Lukas, Gloria Stuart, Edward Arnold, and Onslow Stevens.

"The Secret of the Chateau." In: *Boy's Cinema,* No. 796 (March 16, 1935), 13–20, 27.
  "The first book ever printed, the Gutenberg Bible, rouses the greed and passions of those coveting its possession. In the eerie old chateau where the bible is kept, strange things happen, and Marotte, the great detective, is baffled. A gripping thriller, starring Clark Williams and Claire Dodd." Seven photos from the 1934 Universal film. Credits on page 26; George E. Stone also in cast.

"Secrets of Wu Sin." In: *The Film Star Weekly,* Vol. 3, No. 55 (December 9, 1933), 5–7, 25.
  "A story of daring adventure and death in the haunts of the yellow man." Two photos from the Universal film with Lois Wilson and Grant Withers.

Seven Footprints to Satan. By A. Merritt. New York: Grosset & Dunlap, c. 1928.
  Eight photos from the 1929 First National movie with Thelma Todd and Creighton Hale.

Seven Keys to Baldpate. By Earl Derr Biggers. New York: Grosset & Dunlap, c. 1913.
  Four photos from the 1926 Paramount picture starring Douglas MacLean. Front cover has dye-ink drawing of seven keys.

Seven Keys to Baldpate. By Earl Derr Biggers. New York: Grosset & Dunlap, c. 1913.
Eight photos from the 1929 RKO Richard Dix movie, with additional colored drawing from the film on dust jacket. Front cover has dye-ink drawing of seven keys.

Seven Keys to Baldpate see *10 Classic Mystery and Suspense Plays*

The Seventh Voyage of Sinbad. Dell comic No. 944. New York: Dell Publishing Co., Inc., 1958.
Comic book version of the 1958 Columbia Pictures film, with color photo of Kerwin Mathews on cover and five b&w photos on inside front cover (with film credits). Color "Map of Colossa" on back cover. Special effects by Ray Harryhausen.

70,000 Witnesses: A Football Mystery. By Cortland Fitzsimmons. New York: Grosset & Dunlap, 1931.
Four internal photos from the 1932 Paramount mystery with Phillips Holmes as Buck Buchan and Dorothy Jordan as Dorothy Clark.

She. By H. Rider Haggard. New York: Grosset & Dunlap, 1926.
Eight photos from the 1925 Lee Bradford Production with Betty Blythe. Additional color artwork on dust jacket.

She. By H. Rider Haggard. London: Hodder and Stoughton, "completely reset: 1925; Fourteenth impression: August, 1949."
Dust jacket (only) has one colored photo of Helen Gahagan from the 1935 Merian C. Cooper RKO production.

She. By H. Rider Haggard. New York: Lancer Books, 1965. No. 72–925.
Full color photo of Ursula Andress on front cover; three additional monotone color photos on back cover, from the Seven Arts–Hammer Picture.

Sherlock Holmes. By A. Conan Doyle. New York: R. F. Fenno & Company, 1903.
Ten photos from the stage production with William Gillette as Holmes; most show actors in costume but not stage sets. (Exception is photo facing page 200, similar to frontispiece of *Tales of Sherlock Holmes* [below].) Front cover has dye-ink drawing of Gillette as Holmes (compare to photo facing page 163). This volume is very similar to *Original Adventures of Sherlock Holmes* (see entry); dissimilar to *Tales of Sherlock Holmes*, below, with different Gillette photos.

"Sherlock Holmes." Fictionized by West Peterson. In: *Screen Romances*, Vol. 18, No. 125 (October 1939), 42–44, 60–62.
Four photos from the 1939 20th Century–Fox film *The Adventures of Sherlock Holmes* with Basil Rathbone, Nigel Bruce, Ida Lupino, and George Zucco.

Sherlock Holmes see *Adventures of Sherlock Holmes; Baker Street;* "Dressed to Kill," *The Hound of the Baskervilles; Murder by Decree; Original Adventures of Sherlock Holmes; A Study in Terror; Tales of Sherlock Holmes*

"Sherlock Holmes and the Secret Weapon." Fictionized by Anita Philips. In: *Screen Romances*, Vol. 28, No. 165 (February 1943), 38–39, 89–90.
"Dr. Franz Tobel's rescue was only the beginning of an adventure which nearly cost Sherlock Holmes his life!" Four photos from the Universal Production with Basil Rathbone, Nigel Bruce, and Lionel Atwill as "Moriarity" [*sic*].

"Sherlock Holmes and the Voice of Terror." Fictionized by Helen McCloy. In: *Screen Romances,* Vol. 27, No. 162 (November 1942), 39, 79.
Two photos from the 1942 Universal film, showing Basil Rathbone, Nigel Bruce, Evelyn Ankers, and Reginald Denny.

"A Shot in the Dark." In: *Boy's Cinema*, No. 815 (July 27, 1935), 3–10.
"A grim tapping against a window of a college in the early hours of the morning reveals a tragedy. A clever detective sets out to solve the baffling mystery; several people are under suspicion and a student who knows something is forced to keep silent. Who is the killer?" Cover plus six internal photos from the 1935 Chesterfield film with Charles Starret and Edward Van Sloan. Masked killer in deserted house plot; Van Sloan character is the murderer. Credits on page 2. (The same issue has "Murder on a Honeymoon.")

The Silent House. By John G. Brandon. London: The Readers Library Publishing Company Ltd., April 1930 printing. No. 156.
"Illustrated edition" on color artwork dust jacket showing green skeleton reaching from behind yellow idol to grab red-haired woman around her throat; bat flies nearby. Back cover of jacket shows yellow-skinned Chan Fu figure with outstretched hands; another bat flies nearby. Dark, silhouetted house in background of both front and back. Eight photos appear internally, on four double-sided sheets, from the 1929 film. Title page reads: "The book of the famous play by John G. Brandon and George Pickett / An Archibald Nettlefold Production Distributed by Butchers Film Service Ltd. / Starring: Gibb McLaughlin and Mabel Poulton."

The Silent House. By John G. Brandon. London: The Readers Library Publishing Company Ltd., n.d. [1929?]. [No number; different from No. 156 above].

Without dust jacket; no illustrations. Title page says, "The book of the famous play by John G. Brandon and George Pickett." Preface says: "So confident of the popularity of *The Silent House* are its theatrical producers that they themselves are going to produce a film of the story." This became a 1929 silent film with Gibb McLaughlin as the Oriental menace Chan Fu.

Silver Screen— 'Invisible Man's Revenge."

Sinbad and the Eye of the Tiger. Novelization by John Ryder Hall, from the screenplay by Beverly Cross. Story by Ray Harryhausen and Beverly Cross. New York: A Kangaroo Book, Published by Pocket Books, 1977. No. 80933.

Color artwork cover shows characters and creatures from the Columbia Pictures movie; back cover gives film credits. Special effects by Ray Harryhausen.

The Skull of the Marquis de Sade and Other Stories. By Robert Bloch. New York: Pyramid Books, First Printing, October 1965. No. R-1247.

Front cover has photo of Peter Cushing looking through magnifying glass at skull. Back cover says, "See THE SKULL—now a shock-filled Paramount motion picture starring Peter Cushing, Christopher Lee and Patrick Wymark. Produced by Max J. Rosenberg and Milton Subotsky."

"Son of Frankenstein." In: *Look Magazine*, Vol. 3, No. 5 (February 28, 1939), 39–41.

Three-page story of the 1939 Universal film told in sequence of 15 captioned photos, with additional close-up of Karloff as the monster.

"Song of the Thin Man." In: *Movie Story Magazine*, Vol. 24, No. 162 (October 1947), 40–43, 64–68.

Five photos from the MGM film with William Powell, Myrna Loy, Keenan Wynn, and Jane Meadows; picture on page 41 is partially colored. Page 68 also has a column, "On the Set of *Song of the Thin Man*," with an additional photo of Powell, Loy, and Asta.

The Sorrows of Satan. By Marie Corelli. New York: A. L. Burt Company, c. 1923.

Four photos from the 1926 Paramount movie.

Sorry, Wrong Number. By Allan Ullman & Lucille Fletcher. New York: Bantam Books, September 1948. No. 356.

Inside note reads: "About The Cover: *She held the phone, staring at it, staring in horror at the cluttered night table. What had she just heard? It couldn't be—it just couldn't be. It was some trick of her imagination ...* Artist Gilbert Darling painted the dramatic cover illustration, taking as his model the beautiful Barbara Stanwyck, starring with Burt Lancaster in the Hal Wallis production, *Sorry, Wrong Number*, released by Paramount Pictures." Back cover has photos of Stanwyck and Lancaster.

"The Spanish Cape Mystery." In: *Boy's Cinema*, No. 850 (March 28, 1936), 13–20, 28.

"Seeking a much needed holiday, a famous detective goes to the Spanish Cape, and in the bungalow he has rented he finds a girl gagged and bound. Within the next few days three people are done to death, and not till the detective thinks the girl is in danger will he take up the case. Starring Donald Cook [as Ellery Queen] and Helen Twelvetrees." Five photos from the 1935 Liberty Pictures film. (The same issue has "The Last Days of Pompeii.")

Speaking of Murder. By Audrey and William Roos. New York: Random House, 1957.

Three photos from the stage production with Lorne Greene and Estelle Winwood.

Spellbound. By Francis Beeding. Cleveland and New York: The World Publishing Company, 1945.

Endpapers have eight photos from the 1945 Alfred Hitchcock movie with Gregory Peck and Ingrid Bergman; dust jacket has seven more. "A Selznick International Picture released through United Artists."

The Spider. By Grace Oursler. New York: Grosset & Dunlap, c. 1929.

Four photos from the stage production.

"The Spider." In: *Movie Story Magazine*, Vol. 20, No. 141 (January 1946), 58, 102–106.

One photo from the 1945 20th Century–Fox film with Richard Conte, Faye Marlowe, Kurt Kreuger, Martin Kosleck, and Mantan Moreland. Credits on page 58 say "based on a play by Charles Fulton Oursler and Lowell Brentano"; minimal resemblance to original story.

"The Spider Woman Strikes Back." In: *Movie Story Magazine*, Vol. 21, No. 145 (May 1946), 46–47, 120–27.

"This couldn't be happening—not in the twentieth century. Human vampires, ghouls—they didn't exist, not even modern style. But this wasn't just a fantastic nightmare—." Three photos from the Universal film with Gale Sondergaard, Brenda Joyce, and Rondo Hatton.

The Spiral Staircase. By Ethel Lina White. Cleveland and New York: The World Publishing Company, 1946.
Title page, three double-sided pages, and endpapers have photos from the 1946 RKO Radio Picture with Dorothy McGuire. Dust jacket has six more photos.

"The Spiral Staircase." Fictionized by Lorraine Stevens. In: *Screen Romances*, Vol. 28, No. 201 (February 1946), 42–44, 86 88–92, 94.
Seven photos from the RKO Radio Picture with Dorothy McGuire, George Brent, and Ethel Barrymore. Full page ad on page 17.

Spirits of the Dead see *Fantastic Tales*

The Splendid Crime see *The Public Defender*

Star Wars: From the Adventures of Luke Skywalker. A novel by George Lukas. New York: Ballantine Books, 1976. No. 26079.
Sixteen glossy pages bound in with color photos and commentary on characters from the 20th Century–Fox movie. Front cover has color poster art.

"Steady Company." By George W. Rogers. In: *Moving Picture Stories*, Vol. 6, No. 133 (July 16, 1915), 18–21.
"Story by Julius Grinnel Furthmann—Scenario by Ida May Parke—Produced by Joseph de Grasse." Lon Chaney appears in two of the four photos from this Rex Film. (The same issue has Chaney in "The Violin Maker.")

The Strange Case of Dr. Jekyll and Mr. Hyde and Other Stories. By Robert Louis Stevenson. New York: Editions for the Armed Service, Inc., n. d. Armed Service Edition No. 885.
Front cover shows reduced image of hardcover book with dust jacket showing Fredric March as both Jekyll and Hyde.

The Strange Case of Mary Page. By Frederick Lewis. New York: Grosset & Dunlap, c. 1916.

Four photos from the 1916 Essanay serial with Edna Mayo; four artwork plates by Fanny Munsell.

The Stranglers of Bombay. By Stuart James. Based on an original screenplay by David Z. Goodman. Derby, Connecticut: Monarch Books, Inc., 1960. No. MM601.
Front and back covers have brownish-tinted photos from the Hammer Film Production/Columbia Pictures Release.

A Study in Terror. By Ellery Queen. New York: Lancer Books, Inc., 1966. No. 73–469.
Front cover has artwork of terrified woman's face, and scalpel. Credits for the Columbia Pictures film are given on the first page. John Neville plays Sherlock Holmes.

The Suspect: Motion Picture Title of "This Way Out." By James Ronald (dust jacket); title page reads *This Way Out.* New York: Grosset & Dunlap, 1930.
Dust jacket (only) has photos of Charles Laughton and Ella Raines on front cover, from the 1944 Universal movie.

The Sword and the Dragon. Dell Movie Classic comic No. 1118. New York: Dell Publishing Co., Inc., 1960.
Front cover has two color photos from the film, of hero fighting dragon, and color inset of bearded figure. Inside front cover has five b&w photos, including one of three-headed dragon, and Vitalite Corp. film credits.

Tales From The Crypt. A Novel by Jack Oleck. Adapted from the screenplay by Milton Subotsky. Based on stories written by Al Feldstein, Johnny Craig and Bill Gaines. New York: Bantam Books, April 1972. No. S7439.
Cover has photo of skull with eyeball; back cover has four color photos from Amicus film with Peter Cushing.

Tales of Mystery and Imagination. By Edgar Allan Poe. London: Pan Books Ltd., eighth printing, 1963. No. G321.
Back cover has yellow-tinted photo of Vincent Price, Mark Damon, and Myrna Fahey from the 1960 American-International/Roger Corman film variously titled *House of Usher* and *The Fall of the House of Usher.*

Tales of Sherlock Holmes. By A. Conan Doyle. New York: Grosset & Dunlap., n.d.
Brown textured cover with elaborate red and black inlay design, title in impressed gold lettering; apparently intended not to be covered by dust

jacket. Pages deckle edged at side and bottom. Eight photos from the William Gillette stage play, including the four from the printing below, but this earlier copy's photos are much sharper. Advertisements at back of book are also different from the copy below.

Tales of Sherlock Holmes. By A. Conan Doyle. New York: Grosset & Dunlap, n.d.
   Reddish cloth cover with simple orange lettering. Four photos from stage production with William Gillette. Apparently a cheaper reprinting of copy above; photos not as sharp. Ads at back refer to (missing) dust jacket.

Tales of Sherlock Holmes. By A. Conan Doyle. New York: Grosset & Dunlap, n.d.
   Front cover of dust jacket (only) has one photo of Basil Rathbone, in deerstalker hat, as Holmes.

Tales of Terror see *Edgar Allan Poe's Tales of Terror* and *Poe's Tales of Terror*

"Tarzan." In: *Screen Romances*, Vol. 6, No. 35 (April 1932), 46–49, 100–102.
   Four photos from the MGM film with Johnny Weissmuller, Maureen O'Sullivan, and C. Aubrey Smith. (No author credit for the fictionization is given, only the note "Based on the story by Edgar Rice Burroughs." The same issue has "Arsene Lupin.")

"Tarzan and His Mate." Fictionized by A. E. Applegate. In: *Screen Romances*, Vol. 10, No. 56 (January 1934), 52–54.
   Five photos from the MGM film with Johnny Weissmuller and Maureen O'Sullivan in very brief fictionization of the story. (The same issue has "The Kennel Murder Case.")

Tarzan and the Golden Lion. By Edgar Rice Burroughs. New York: Grosset & Dunlap, c. 1924.
   Four photos from the 1927 movie with James Pierce and Dorothy Dunbar, "Distributed by Film Booking Offices of America, Inc." (Boris Karloff had a small role in this film, but does not appear in these photos.)

The Teeth of the Tiger. By Maurice Leblanc. Translated by Alexander Teixeira de Mattos. New York: Grosset & Dunlap, c. 1914.
   "Illustrated with Scenes From The Photoplay—Paramount Artcraft Picture—Featuring David Powell." Four internal photos from the 1919 Famous Players–Lasky Corp.'s Arsene Lupin mystery; dust jacket front panel shows brown-tinted photo from movie, with Marguerite Courtout (as Florence Chandler) filing handcuff off Powell/Lupin. The four internal photos do

not correspond to the page numbers or descriptions given in the "List of Illustrations" after the Contents page.

Tell It to the Marines. By E. Richard Schayer. New York: Jacobsen-Hodgkinson Corporation, n.d. Paperback.
   Photos from the 1926 MGM film, with Lon Chaney, on front and back inside and outside covers; one glossy photo bound in; also seven more photos appearing on regular newsprint pages. Front cover in color.

Temple Tower. By H. C. McNeil. Garden City, New York: Published for The Crime Club, Inc., by Doubleday, Doran & Company, Inc., 1929.
   Four internal photos from the 1930 Fox movie with Kenneth MacKenna as Bulldog Drummond (his photo opposite page 232), Marceline Day, and Henry B. Walthall.

10 Classic Mystery and Suspense Plays. With prefaces and an Introductory Note by Stanley Richards. New York: Dodd, Mead & Company, 1973.
   Anthology of ten plays illustrated with photos from their stage productions: *Ten Little Indians* by Agatha Christie; *The Desperate Hours* by Joseph Hays; *Hostile Witness* by Jack Roffey; *Kind Lady* by Edward Chodorov; *The Innocents* by William Archibald; *Night Must Fall* by Emlyn Williams; *An Inspector Calls* by J. B. Priestley; *Uncle Harry* by Thomas Job; *Ladies in Retirement* by Edward Percey and Reginald Denham; and *Seven Keys to Baldpate* by George M. Cohan (photo with Cohan, who also starred in 1917 film version).

Ten Little Indians. By Agatha Christie. Formerly titled *And Then There Were None.* New York: Pocket Books, 41st Printing, March 1975. No. 80151.
   Front cover has artwork poster showing ten stars of the Avco Embassy Release film with Oliver Reed, Elke Sommer, Richard Attenborough, Herbert Lom; small artwork scene of characters surrounding woman's body also on front cover. Back cover gives film credits.

The Terror. By Edgar Wallace. [Glasgow]: Published by the Detective Story Club Ltd. for Wm. Collins Sons & Co. Ltd., n.d.
   Tie-in to the first talkie horror film, released by Warner Bros. in 1928. No internal photos, but there are ten wonderfully atmospheric woodcut pictures of scenes from the story, possibly based on photos from the play or film. "Editor's Preface" says, "This wonderful story has thrilled the London theatre world in its dramatized form; it has been made into a super film, which was one of the first 'talkies' shown to the public, and which will long be pronounced one of the best, and now in book form the Detec-

tive Story Club presents it to the world." Color laser-copy dust jacket shows hooded figure carrying girl down stairs; back cover shows hooded figure with raised arms terrorizing the same girl in front of large pipe organ. Inside flap of dust jacket says, "A sensational success as a play, it has been made into an exciting film, and now comes the book to provide hours of wonderful reading for all who enjoy a first-rate detective story in Edgar Wallace's characteristic style. Follow the unraveling of the mystery of the lonely house throughout whose dark corridors echoed the strange notes of a church organ. Where did it come from and who played it? Who was the hooded form which swept down in the night unseen upon its prey and dragged its victims to destruction?" The Epilogue of *Horror in Silent Films* says, "Adapted from a derivative mystery play by Edgar Wallace, *The Terror* dealt with a *Phantom of the Opera*–type maniac who terrorizes guests in an isolated English mansion.... This film was the first synchronized sound movie of its type, and remains significant, if only for this historical fact."

The Terror see "Return of The Terror"

"Terror Island." By Arthur B. Reeve and John Gray; Adapted from the Photoplay by D. Burton Howard. In: *Moving Picture Stories*, Vol. 15, No. 381 (April 16, 1920), 1–5.
 Two photos from the Paramount-Artcraft Film with Harry Houdini and Lila Lee, directed by James Cruze. Note "Gray" rather than "Grey" is the spelling here; Reeve and Grey also collaborated on the Houdini serial *The Mastery Mystery*.

"Thank You, Mr. Moto." Fictionized by Faith Fenwick. In: *Screen Romances*, Vol. 17, No. 105 (February 1938), 34–37, 124–26.
 Six photos from the 20th Century–Fox film with Peter Lorre and John Carradine.

Thank You, Mr. Moto & Mr. Moto Is So Sorry from the Saturday Evening Post. By J. P. Marquand. Indianapolis, Ind.: The Curtis Publishing Company, 1977.
 Reprint of 1936 and 1938 stories; dust jacket has one photo of Peter Lorre as Mr. Moto.

They Came From Outer Space: 12 Classic Science Fiction Tales that Became Major Motion Pictures. Edited by Jim Wynorski. Introduction by Ray Bradbury. Garden City, N.Y.: Doubleday & Company, Inc., c. 1980.
 Anthology of stories illustrated with photos from their respective

movies: *Dr. Cyclops* by Henry Kuttner; *Who Goes There? (The Thing from Another World)* by John W. Campbell; *Farewell to the Master (The Day the Earth Stood Still)* by Harry Bates; *The Fog Horn (The Beast from 20,000 Fathoms)* by Ray Bradbury; *Deadly City (Target Earth)* by Ivar Jorgenson; *The Alien Machine (This Island Earth)* by Raymond F. Jones; *The Cosmic Frame (Invasion of the Saucermen)* by Paul W. Fairman; *The Fly* by George Langelaan; *The Seventh Victim (The Tenth Victim)* by Robert Sheckley; *The Sentinel (2001: A Space Odyssey)* by Arthur C. Clarke; *The Racer (Death Race 2000)* by Ib Melchior; and *A Boy and His Dog* by Harlan Ellison.

"They Might Be Giants." Adapted by Jean Francis Webb. In: *Screen Stories*, Vol. 69, No. 11 (November 1969), 30–33, 70–78.
Six photos from the Universal film with George C. Scott and Joanne Woodward.

They Might Be Giants. By James Goldman. New York: Lancer Books, 1970. No. 74740–075.
Script of the 1970 Universal film with George C. Scott and Joanne Woodward. Cover photos of the two stars, and seven internal photos.

The Thief of Bagdad. By Achmed Abdullah. London: Hutchinson & Co., n.d. Third Edition. 252 pp.
Same four photos from the Fairbanks movie as in the A. L. Burt edition, but different typography, pagination and binding.

The Thief of Bagdad. By Achmed Abdullah. London: The Readers Library Publishing Company Ltd., n.d. [No. 131 reprint, 1925, in Richard Williams' *Readers Library* bibliography.]
Colored dust jacket has artwork of Thief leaning over woman in bed. No internal illustrations. Editor's note refers to Douglas Fairbanks film.

The Thief of Bagdad. By Achmed Abdullah. New York: A. L. Burt Company, c. 1924. 310 pp. plus 10 page list of "Popular Copyright Novels."
Four photos from the 1924 Douglas Fairbanks movie.

"The Thief of Bagdad." Fictionized by David Frazer. In: *Screen Romances*, Vol. 23, No. 139 (December 1940), 31, 62–65.
Two photos showing Sabu, John Justin and June Duprez from Alexander Korda's 1940 United Artists film. (The same issue has "You'll Find Out.")

"The Thin Man." [Anon. author] In: *Screen Romances*, Vol. 11, No. 63 (August 1934), 70–71.

Four photos from the MGM film, accompanying very brief plot summary, including the name of the murderer. (The same issue has "Return of The Terror.")

"The Thin Man." Fictionized by T. R. Carskadon. In: *Romantic Movie Stories*, Vol. 1, No. 10 (September 1934), 38–41, 77–79.
Eight photos from MGM film with William Powell and Myrna Loy; also artwork of Thin Man in coat and hat. Full story is given, including the name of the murderer. Page 39 reproduces a handwritten note from Powell:

> After some of the "stuffed shirts" I have endeavored to characterize in the past, I found it a joy to play "Nick Charles". My sincere thanks go to Metro-Goldwyn-Mayer and a very low bow to Dashiell Hammett and W. S. Van Dyke.
>
> William Powell

(Powell may be alluding to his previous characterizations of Philo Vance.)

"The Thin Man." In: *Boy's Cinema*, No. 768 (September 1, 1934), 1–8, 25–27.
"A detective, who has married a rich girl and retired, refuses persistently to be dragged into a strange mystery, but the case is so baffling that in the end he becomes interested and involved. Starring William Powell and Myrna Loy." Nine photos from the MGM film; cast credits on page 25.

"The Thin Man Goes Home." Fictionized by Helen McCloy. In: *Screen Romances*, Vol. 28, No. 189 (February 1945), 40–43, 74–77.
Seven photos from the MGM film.

[*Things to Come*] "A Guide to the Discussion of the Photoplay *Things to Come* Based on a Scenario by H. G. Wells." Prepared by Alfred F. Mayhew. *Photoplay Studies*, Vol. 2, No. 4 (April 1936).
Sixteen page reprint pamphlet with eight photos from the 1936 William Cameron Menzies film with Raymond Massey. Cast and credits listing is given on page 14.

"Think Fast, Mr. Moto!" Fictionized by Ann Silver. In: *Screen Romances*, Vol. 17, No. 99 (August 1937), 80–82, 116–20.
Five photos from the 1937 20th Century–Fox film with Peter Lorre, Sig Rumann, and J. Carroll Naish. (Table of contents omits exclamation point.)

"Think Fast, Mr. Moto." In: *Boy's Cinema*, No. 938 (December 4, 1937), 15–18, 28.
"Diamond smugglers are using a certain steamship line to transport contraband. The son of the owner is sent with a confidential letter to Shang-

hai and becomes involved with a mysterious Jap, a beautiful girl and a villainous Russian in a strange adventure. Starring Peter Lorre." Five photos from the 20th Century–Fox film. Credits on p. 27.

13. By Philip Lorraine. Originally published as *Day of the Arrow.* New York: Lancer Books, 1966. No. 73–540.
Cover has one photograph of Deborah Kerr from the MGM film.

The Thirteenth Chair: A Play in Three Acts. By Bayard Veiller. New York: Samuel French, 1922.
Three photos from the 1916 New York stage production at the 48th Street Theatre.

"The Thirteenth Chair." Fictionized by Ann Silver. In: *Screen Romances,* Vol. 17, No. 98 (July 1937), 66–68, 109–112.
Four photos from the 1937 MGM mystery.

"The Thirteenth Guest." In: *Screen Stories,* No. 143 (October 29, 1932), 1–8, 26–27.
"An elusive mystery story that will grip you and thrill you to the last. Starring Ginger Rogers, Lyle Talbot, and J. Farrell MacDonald." Five photos, including front cover, from the Monogram Pictures Corp. film; credits on page 25. The same issue has Episode 11 of "The Air Mail Mystery" serial. Back cover includes interesting advertisement for:

BOY DETECTIVE DISGUISE OUTFITS,

containing Grease Paints (Sallow or Chinese, Sunburn or Red Indian); Moustaches; Hair (assorted colors); Removable Scars and Warts; Toothblack enamel; etc. TWELVE ITEMS, including useful book, "Secrets of Disguise," only 1/6. Or larger, with extra Grease Paints, Monocle, Beard, etc., 2/6.

"The 13th Guest." In: *The Film Star Weekly and Girl's Cinema,* Vol. 1, No. 6 (December 31, 1932), 12–20, 22.
"A vast inheritance—left to the thirteenth guest at a dinner party table— led to jealousy, threats and even murder by others who desired to get hold of the money." Three photos from the 1932 Monogram film with Ginger Rogers and Lyle Talbot. Credits on page 18.

The 13th Hour. By Sydney Horler. London: The Readers Library Publishing Company Ltd., n.d. [1928] [No. 224].
Eight internal b&w photos, on four double-sided glossy pages, from the 1927 MGM movie with Lionel Barrymore, including one of Barrymore out

of character. (Second copy has six photos.) Title page reads, "The 13th Hour: A Chilling, Thrilling Mystery ... Illustrated with Scenes from the Photo-Play / A Metro-Goldwyn-Mayer Production Starring Lionel Barrymore And Jacqueline Gadson / The Book of the Film." One photo is of clutching hand reaching for frightened woman: "Through the thick curtains a naked hand and arm appeared." Old house mystery with masked and cloaked killer, secret passages and rooms, imprisoning chair, chair dumping occupant into hidden room, semi-Oriental servant. Features Rex, an heroic Alsatian dog.

The Thirty-Nine Steps see *Modern Mystery and Adventure Novels*

This Gun for Hire. By Grahame Greene. New York: Triangle Books, 1942.
    Dust jacket has three photos from the 1942 Paramount film with Alan Ladd and Veronica Lake.

This Way Out see *The Suspect*

The 3 Worlds of Gulliver. Dell Movie Classic comic No. 1158. New York: Dell Publishing Co., Inc., 1960.
    Comic book version of the 1960 Columbia Pictures film. Front cover has color photo; inside front cover has five b&w photos and screen credits. Special effects by Ray Harryhausen.

"The Three Worlds of Gulliver." By George Scullin. In: *Screen Stories*, Vol. 60, No. 1 (January 1961), 28–31, 38–40.
    Three photos from the 1960 Columbia Pictures production with Kerwin Mathews; special effects by Ray Harryhausen.

The 3 Worlds of Gulliver see *Gulliver's Travels*

Thrilling Wonder Stories— "Dr. Cyclops."

"Ticket to a Crime." In: *Boy's Cinema*, No. 803 (May 4, 1935), 13–19, 28.
    "A man is found murdered at the Lido Country Club, and although several people are under suspicion the police cannot find the culprit; but Clay Holt, private detective, and his pretty secretary unearth the one vital clue and bring the murderer to justice. A thrilling drama, starring Ralph Graves and Lola Lane." Six photos, one captioned, from the 1934 Beacon Productions film: "He turned to meet a shadowy masked figure who silently sprang at him." Credits on page 2.

The Time Machine. By H.G. Wells. New York: A Berkley Medallion Book
  published by the Berkley Publishing Corporation, Second Edition, September, 1960. Medallion No. G445.
  Front cover artwork; back cover has two b&w photos of Rod Taylor and
  a Morlock from the MGM George Pal production.

The Time of Their Lives see "The Ghost Steps Out"

Tomb of Ligeia. Dell Movie Classic Comic No. 12-830-506. New York:
  Dell Publishing Co., Inc., 1965.
  Comic book version. Front cover has color artwork of Vincent Price;
  inside front cover has movie credits and four b&w photos from the 1965
  American-International Picture, and film credits.

"To-morrow at Seven." In: *Boy's Cinema*, No. 720 (September 30, 1933),
  3-12, 26-28.
  "A young novelist who specializes in crime stories sets out to discover a
  real murderer who has baffled the police for a long time—and gets caught
  up in his toils, other crimes being committed even after two blundering
  detectives have joined in the chase. A mystery yarn on entirely new lines."
  Ten photos (including cover) from Radio Pictures mystery with Chester
  Morris, Frank McHugh, Allen Jenkins, and Charles Middleton. Credits
  on page 2. (The same issue has a preview photo of Lionel Atwill, Gloria
  Stuart, and Paul Lukas from "Secrets of the Blue Room," advertised as
  appearing in the next issue.)

"Topper Returns." Fictionized by Robert Arthur. In: *Screen Romances*, Vol.
  24. No. 142 (March 1941), 34-36, 73-75.
  Four photos from the United Artists mystery-ghost story-comedy with
  Joan Blondell, Roland Young, Carole Landis, H. B. Warner, Patsy Kelly,
  and George Zucco.

"Tower of London." In: *Movie Story Magazine*, Vol. 14, No. 67 (December
  1939), 48-50, 90-96.
  Seven photos, plus tapestry and shield backgrounds, from the Universal
  picture with Basil Rathbone, Vincent Price, and Boris Karloff. An additional photo of Rathbone appears in the table of contents, page 4.

Treasure Island. By Robert Louis Stevenson. New York: Grosset & Dunlap, n.d.
  Four pages of photos, preceding title page, from the 1935 MGM film
  with Jackie Coogan and Wallace Beery.

Treasure Island. By Robert Louis Stevenson. New York: The Charles Renard
   Company, Publishers, 1925.
   Illustrations list says, "The Publishers are indebted to the Famous Players–Lasky Corporation for their courtesy in furnishing the sixteen Life Portraits which comprise a part of this volume." The sixteen photos from the
1920 film appear on eight double-sided glossy inserts. Charles Ogle plays
Long John Silver (Ogle played the Frankenstein monster in the 1910 Edison production; photos opposite pp. 9, 24, 25, 72). Lon Chaney plays two
roles, Pew (photos opposite pp. 24, 73) and Merry (photos opposite pp.
184, 185). Bull Montana plays Tom Morgan (Montana went on to play the
apeman in the 1925 *Lost World*; photos opposite pp. 73, 137, 153, 184, 185).
Photo opposite p. 25 shows Ogle and Chaney together; photos opposite
73, 184, 185 show Chaney and Montana together.

Treasure Island. By Robert Louis Stevenson. Toronto: The Copp Clark Co.,
   Limited, 1926.
   Frontispiece is photo of Stevenson; photo opposite page 67 is of
Swanston Cottage, his boyhood home. Photos on pages 106 and 137 are
from the 1920 Famous Players–Lasky Corporation film. The picture on
page 137 shows Lon Chaney at the top of the stockade, gesturing others
to follow, with Bull Montana grasping the fence pole with both hands.
(Attributions based on clearer pictures of costumes and make-up in the
above Renard edition.)

20 Million Miles to Earth. By Henry Slesar. Amazing Stories Science Fiction Novel. New York: Ziff-Davis Publishing Co., 1957. Paperback.
   Eight b&w drawings based on scenes from the 1957 Columbia Pictures
movie, plus color artwork on cover, and b&w movie poster containing photo
on inside front cover. Special effects by Ray Harryhausen.

20,000 Leagues Under the Sea. By Jules Verne. New York: Grosset & Dunlap, c. 1917.
   Eight photos from the 1916 Universal film. (Variant edition has four
photos.) Dye-ink artwork of submarine on cover.

20,000 Leagues Under the Sea. By Jules Verne. New York: Grosset & Dunlap, c. 1917. Every Boy's Library Boy Scout Edition.
   Eight photos from the 1916 Universal film (the same eight as above), with
dye-ink artwork of Boy Scout badge (eagle with motto "Be Prepared") on
cover and spine. The frontispiece and title page in this edition are preceded
by a two-page letter "TO THE PUBLIC" by James E. West, "Chief Scout
Executive," dated July 31, 1913; it reads, in part:

In the execution of its purpose to give educational value and moral worth to the recreational activities of the boyhood of America, the leaders of the Boy Scout Movement quickly learned that to effectively carry out its purposes, the boy must be influenced not only in his out-of-door life but also in the diversions of his other leisure moments. It is at such times that the boy is captured by the tales of daring enterprises and adventurous good times. What now is needful is not that this taste should be thwarted but trained. There should constantly be presented to him the books the boy likes best, yet always the books that will be best for the boy. As a matter of fact, however, the boy's taste is being constantly vitiated and exploited by the great mass of cheap juvenile literature.

To help anxiously concerned parents and educators to meet this grave peril, the Library Commission of the Boy Scouts of America has been organized. EVERY BOY'S LIBRARY is the result of their labors.

20,000 Leagues Under the Sea. Dell Movie Classic comic No. 614. New York: Dell Publishing Co., Inc., 1954.

Comic book version of the Walt Disney production. Front cover has color artwork from movie; inside front cover has four b&w photos. No film credits given; story panels continue onto back cover.

"20,000 Leagues Under the Sea." Fictionization by Jean Francis Webb. In: *Screen Stories*, Vol. 53, No. 1 (January 1955), 29–33, 77–80.

Thirteen photos from the Walt Disney production with Kirk Douglas, James Mason, Paul Lukas, and Peter Lorre.

Twice Told Tales see *Nathaniel Hawthorne's Twice Told Tales*

Uncharted Seas see *The Lost Continent*

"The Unholy Night." By Muriel Thirer. In: *Screen Book Magazine*, Vol. 4, No. 1 (January 1930), 56–64.

"A dead man's lustful desire for revenge results in a night of tragedy and death." Eight photos from the 1929 MGM picture with Roland Young, John Miljan, and Boris Karloff. (Karloff appears in two.) Page 63 has a photo of a séance with spectral apparitions.

The Unholy Three. By C. A. "Tod" Robbins. New York: A. L. Burt Company, c. 1917.

Four photos from the 1925 MGM film with Lon Chaney. Dust jacket front has b&w photo of the three.

The Uninvited. By Dorothy Macardle. New York: Bantam Books, April 1947. No. 90.

Back cover notes that the story "was made into a Paramount picture starring Ray Milland and Ruth Hussey." No photos or artwork from the movie.

"The Uninvited." In: *Movie Story Magazine*, Vol. 17, No. 120 (April 1944), 40–43, 74, 76–81, 83.
Six photos from the 1944 Paramount film with Ray Milland, Ruth Hussey, Gail Russell, Donald Crisp, Cornelia Otis Skinner, and Alan Napier.

"The Uninvited." Fictionized by Allan Ballard. In: *Screen Romances*, Vol. 28, No. 179 (April 1944), 62–63, 77.
One photo from the Paramount film. Full page ad with additional photos appears on page 11.

The Unsuspected. By Charlotte Armstrong. New York: Pocket Books, Inc., 4th printing, September 1947. No. 444.
Front cover has b&w photo of Joan Caulfield, Claude Rains, Audrey Totter and Michael North from the Warner Bros. film.

The Valley of Gwangi. Dell Movie comic No. 01–880–912. New York: Dell Publishing Co., Inc., 1969.
Comic book version of the 1969 Warner Bros.–Seven Arts film. Front cover has color artwork from the movie; inside front cover gives film credits. No photographs. Special effects by Ray Harryhausen.

The Vampire Lovers and Other Stories. By J. Sheridan Le Fanu. London: Collins/Fontana Books, 1970. No. 2457.
Front and back cover have color photos from the American International–Hammer production. The title page of this particular copy is autographed by Ingrid Pitt.

"Vanishing Shadow." In: *Boy's Cinema*, No. 768 (September 1, 1934), 19–23; No. 769 (September 8, 1934), 21–25.
"Stanley Stanfield, seeking to avenge a wrong committed by a crooked political group, invents an Invisible Ray. In the battle which ensues between science and crime, a man-made monster of steel, the Death Ray and the Paralyzing Ray also play a grim part. A really thrilling serial, starring Onslow Stevens and Ada Ince." No. 768: Episode 7, "The Tragic Crash"; No. 769: Episode 8, "The Shadow of Death." Each issue has six photos from the Universal serial, one showing the "man-made monster of steel" robot. (Issue No. 768 also has "The Thin Man"; issue No. 769, "The House of Mystery.")

"The Violin Maker." By Frederick R. Denton. In: *Moving Picture Stories*, Vol. 6, No. 133 (July 16, 1915), 1–5.

"Scenario by Milton M. Moore—Produced by Lon Chaney." Lon Chaney appears in three photos from this 1915 Victor Film; an additional photo is of Frances Nelson. (The same issue has Chaney in "Steady Company.")

Voyage to the Bottom of the Sea. Dell Movie Classic comic No. 1230. New York: Dell Publishing Co., Inc., 1961.

Front cover has color artwork of tentacled beast attacking submarine, and color photo of Peter Lorre, Joan Fontaine, and Barbara Eden from the 20th Century–Fox film. Inside front cover has five b&w photos and film credits.

Voyage to the Bottom of the Sea. By Theodore Sturgeon. New York: Pyramid Books, first printing, June 1961. No. G622.

Cover artwork of submarine and sea monster. Back cover gives screen credits for Irwin Allen 20th Century–Fox production.

Voyage to the Bottom of the Sea. By Theodore Sturgeon. New York: Pyramid Books, second printing, September 1964. No. R-1068.

Front cover has b&w photo from the ABC-TV series; series ad on back cover.

"The Walking Dead." In: *Movie Action Magazine*, 1, 6 (June 1936), 2–25.

Eight b&w internal photos (one split on two pages) from the 1936 Warner Bros. film; five show Karloff, one his shadow. Color artwork on cover shows green Karloff character pursuing four frightened men.

War-Gods of the Deep. Dell Movie Classic comic No. 12–900–509. New York: Dell Publishing Co., Inc., 1965.

Front cover has color photo of large horned god with actress Susan Hart, and inset of Vincent Price from the American-International movie. Inside front cover has 10 b&w photos, and film credits.

The War of the Worlds. By H. G. Wells. London: Heinemann, 1958.

Hardcover; front dust jacket panel (only) has b&w photo of actress Ann Robinson with Martian hand clutching at her shoulder; also colored depictions of two Martian spaceships from George Pal's 1953 Paramount picture.

The War of The Worlds. By H. G. Wells. New York: Pocket Books, Inc., 1st printing, March 1953. No. 947.

Paperback; front cover has color photo of Martian machine against exploding building from George Pal's Paramount movie; back cover has red-tinted copy of the same photo.

"Weird Woman." In: *Movie Story Magazine*, Vol. 17, No. 122 (June 1944), 50, 121–29.
    Short story version of the 1944 Universal "Inner Sanctum Mystery" with Lon Chaney, Anne Gwynne, Evelyn Ankers, Ralph Morgan, and Elizabeth Russell. Two photos of Chaney and Gwynne appear, on pages 50 and 122. Credits on page 50.

"The Werewolf of London." In: *Boy's Cinema*, No. 812 (July 6, 1935), 13–20, 29, 31.
    "Seeking for a rare and mysterious flower in distant Tibet, a clever scientist has a struggle with a strange creature that bites him and escapes. On returning to England with the flower that blooms only under the light of the moon, the scientist learns that he is under a dread spell and when the moon is full he is doomed to change into an evil monstrosity." Seven photos from the 1935 Universal film with Henry Hull, Warner Oland, and Valerie Hobson. Credits on page 29.

Werewolf of London. By Carl Dreadstone. Adapted from the screenplay by John Colton, based upon an original story by Robert Harris. With and introduction by Ramsey Campbell. New York: Berkley Publishing Corporation, 1977.
    Numerous photos from the 1935 Universal movie.

Werewolf vs. Vampire Woman. By Arthur N. Scarm. Beverly Hills, California: Guild-Hartford Publishing Company, Inc., 1972. No. BG 200.
    Front cover has two color photos of Paul Naschy as the Werewolf from the 1970 First Leisure Entertainment Corporation film; back cover has one color photo of Vampire Woman attacking another woman. This particular copy is autographed "Paul Naschy 2000."

The Westland Case see *Headed for a Hearse*

Where East Is East. By Tod Browning and Harry Sinclair Drago. New York: Jacobsen Publishing Co., Inc., c. 1929. Paperback.
    Front cover has color photo/drawing from the 1929 MGM film with Lon Chaney; back cover has b&w artwork of Chaney.

"Whispering Ghosts." In: *Movie Story Magazine*, Vol. 18, No. 98 (June 1942), 38–39, 79–85.

Five photos from the 20th Century–Fox mystery comedy with Milton Berle, Willie Best, and John Carradine. Additional photo of Berle, out of character, appears on page 80.

Whispering Wires. By Henry Leverage. New York: Grosset & Dunlap, c. 1918.
    Four photos from stage production at the 49th St. Theatre.

"Whistling in Brooklyn." Fictionized by Helen Cunningham. In: *Screen Romances*, Vol. 28, No. 174 (November 1943), 26–28, 78–79, 82–86.
    Six photos from the MGM comedy-mystery with Red Skelton (as Wally Benton, "The Fox"), Ann Rutherford, Jean Rogers, "Rags" Ragland, Ray Collins, and the Brooklyn Dodgers.

"Whistling in Dixie." In: *Movie Story Magazine*, Vol. 14, No. 104 (December 1942), 44–45, 61–66.
    Five photos from the MGM film with Red Skelton, Ann Rutherford, and Rags Ragland. (The same issue has "Who Done It?")

"Whistling in the Dark." In: *Movie Story Magazine*, Vol. 17, No. 90 (October 1941), 54, 77–79.
    One photo from the MGM film with Red Skelton, Ann Rutherford, Conrad Veidt, and Rags Ragland.

"Who Done It?" Fictionized by Marjorie Bailey. In: *Screen Romances*, Vol. 27, No. 163 (December 1942), 58, 86.
    One photo of Abbott and Costello from the 1942 Universal mystery-comedy with Patric Knowles and Louise Albritton.

"Who Done It?" In: *Movie Story Magazine*, Vol. 14, No. 104 (December 1942), 36–37, 99–104, 106.
    Five photos from the Universal film with Abbott & Costello, Patric Knowles, Louise Albritton, William Bendix, and Ludwig Stossel. An additional photo of Abbott and Costello, on a bond-selling tour, appears on page 103. (The same issue has "Whistling in Dixie.")

"The Wolf Man." In: *Movie Story Magazine*, Vol. 17, No. 94 (February 1942), 50, 68, 70–74.
    Three photos from the Universal film with Lon Chaney, Evelyn Ankers, Claude Rains, Maria Ouspenskaya. (The same issue has "Mr. and Mrs. North.")

The Woman in the Window (Once Off Guard). By J. H. Wallace. Cleveland

and New York: The World Publishing Company, Tower Books Edition, Second Printing, April 1945.

Dust jacket (only) has five b&w photos from the 1944 International Pictures film with Edward G. Robinson, Joan Bennett, Raymond Massey. Photo on spine duplicates front cover photo; four more on back cover.

The Woman in White. By Wilkie Collins. Cleveland and New York: The World Publishing Company, February 1947.

Dust jacket (only) has scenes from the 1948 Warner Bros. film with Eleanor Parker, Alexis Smith, Sydney Greenstreet, Gig Young; b&w photos against blue-tinted forest background.

"The Wonderful World of the Brothers Grimm." In: *Screen Stories*, Vol. 61, No. 10 (October 1962), 17–23, 57–60.

Eleven photos from the 1962 George Pal MGM film. (The same issue has "The Phantom of the Opera.")

Worlds Unknown Presents The Golden Voyage of Sinbad see *The Golden Voyage of Sinbad* (comic).

X. Adapted by Eunice Sudak from the screenplay by Robert Dillon and Ray Russell. New York: Lancer Books, 1963. No. 70–052.

Front cover has photo of Ray Milland, mostly tinted green, with face left white and eye areas tinted red. Back cover shows orange-tinted photo of lower torso of dancing woman in her underwear; back cover also gives film credits of the American-International Picture.

"X": The Man with the X-Ray Eyes. Gold Key comic No. 10083–309. Poughkeepsie, New York: K.K. Publications, Inc., 1963.

Front and back covers have color artwork; front also has b&w photo of Ray Milland. Inside front cover has five b&w photos from the American-International film, and credits.

"You'll Find Out." Fictionized by West Peterson. In: *Screen Romances*, Vol. 23, No. 139 (December 1940), 30, 71–75.

One photo from the 1940 RKO-Radio film with Kay Kyser. Full-page ad for the film, showing Lugosi, Lorre, and Karloff, appears on page 11. (The same issue has "The Thief of Badgad.")

Young Frankenstein. A novel by Gilbert Pearlman based on the screenplay by Gene Wilder & Mel Brooks. New York: Ballantine Books, 1974. No. 24268.

Sixteen pages of photos bound in; front cover has color poster art; back cover has b&w negative photo from the 20th Century–Fox film. Inside front and back covers have additional b&w photos.

Appendix:
"The Gorilla"

Virginia Brunswick Smith

For weeks an unseen monster had terrorized the great city of New York. Not since the publication of Edgar Allan Poe's story of the murders in the Rue Morgue had such blood-curdling atrocities filled the press, baffled the police and reduced the population to a state of hysteria. The Terror came and went seemingly like a shadow. High walls, bolts, bars, extra watchmen had no deterring effect whatever. Unrecognized, he scaled the most impregnable barriers and slipped past sentries, always with robbery as his motive, always leaving behind one grisly clue—the marks of a massive hand on the strangled throat of his victim, a hand that grotesquely resembled a human being's, but which, by its size and super-human strength, belonged unquestionably to one of the larger simians—by popular consent, to a gorilla.

Though every possessor of a sizeable bank account trembled lest he be the next victim of the Monster, probably no plutocrat in the city had pitted against the nameless criminal such an array of protective devices as had the eccentric recluse, Cyrus Townsend, reputed to be a multimillionaire. The Townsend mansion with its gables and cupola, set fortress-like high on the brink of the Palisades, could be approached only from the side toward the city. Every window toward the river had a sheer drop of 200 feet or more to the flowing Hudson below. Cyrus Townsend's own quarters were in the top of the cupola, accessible by a

This is an adaptation of First National's screen presentation of Ralph Spence's stage play. Al Cohn and Henry McCarthy wrote the scenario and Alfred Santell directed with Charlie Murray appearing as Garrity, Fred Kelsey as Mulligan, Alice Day as Alice Townsend, Tully Marshall as William Townsend, Claude Gillingwater as Cyrus Townsend, Walter Pidgeon as Stevens, Gaston Glass as Marsden, Brooks Benedict as the Reporter, Aggie Herring as the Cook, Syd Corssley as the Butler, and John Gough as the Italian.

They all turned to look with crawling scalps and congealed blood at a horrible apparition standing in the window.

winding stair that communicated with several tiers of libraries and studies, all reserved for his special use, and always bolted and barred from intrusion to all save the members of his immediate household.

This included his only child, Alice, a lovely creature in her 'teens; William Townsend, his dependent brother, even more eccentric than himself; Robert Marsden, his secretary, and Edward Stevens, a youth whom he had befriended and who he hoped would some day succeed in supplanting Robert Marsden in his daughter's affections. Kathie, the cook, and James, the butler, were the only servants allowed above stairs. The rich recluse was becoming suspicious of his own shadow since the unsolved murders by the "Gorilla" had cast a pall over New York.

Notwithstanding his precautions and safeguards, a certain night in October found Cyrus Townsend shaking with dread. Robbery always preceded the mysterious murders, and an examination of his strong box in the wall safe had just shown him that he had been cleaned out. Was it Marsden, the dapper, suave secretary for whom Alice so openly expressed her preference? Was it his brother William, always envious and grasping and counting on dead men's shoes? Or could the butler have found the secret spring that operated the hidden panel behind which the wall safe was built? These were the only three in his family circle on whom the millionaire's suspicions rested—unless it were indeed the Gorilla who had gained access to this apparently inaccessible den of his in the cupola.

A sudden rattle of the window sash—the window set like an eagle's eyrie high above the river! No human being could have scaled that blank wall! Not daring to turn around, Cyrus Townsend was aware that *something* had entered the room behind him, was creeping up the circular staircase from the room below. Suddenly a reflection shone for a moment in the burnished brass plate on the desk, and the millionaire knew his hour had come.

He did not betray himself. With masterly self-control he sat down and feverishly wrote a note to his daughter, crossed to the secret panel where he hid it safely, and then—

The only evidence to show how death had come to the tenth victim of the Gorilla was the mark upon Cyrus Townsend's throat of four hairy fingers.

"Send for the police. Let no one leave the house!" Young Stevens took command of the situation when the first cries of horror had died away. Alice and Robert Marsden had just returned from the theatre when Stevens rushed down from the cupola to announce the awful news. The cook and butler were clinging to each other like frightened children. Not a word was uttered by the group who stood staring down at the stiffening form of the master of the house. The clock ticked off the lagging moments. Would the police never come?

Alice stirred restlessly and glanced down at the desk. Then, with a wild shriek, she flung herself into Marsden's arms. Almost under her hand as it rested on the desk top lay a warning.

"Do not try to catch the Gorilla. It can't be done. But at midnight he will return. And no one left in the house at that hour will live to tell the tale."

Every eye flew to the clock. It was quarter to twelve.

"How did that warning get on the table?" demanded William Townsend, glaring at Marsden. "The hand that put it there is the hand that murdered my brother."

"Do you mean to insinuate that Mr. Marsden had anything to do with it?" shrieked Alice indignantly.

"I want to go home!" blubbered the butler. "I don't want to stay here to be done in by the Gorilla."

Five minutes ticked away. Stevens moved nervously but no one wished to take responsibility of advising a general exodus.

"There must be a clue somewhere." Alice wrung her hands.

"I want to go home," wailed the butler. "This place ain't healthy."

William Townsend crossed to the window where the torn curtains showed that a struggle of some kind had taken place.

"Only a man with a flying machine could ever have gotten in that way," he muttered, with a shuddering look at the black waters far below.

Another five minutes was tolled off by the inexorable timepiece.

"Are we all going to stay here and be killed deader than door nails?" whimpered the cook. "I don't blame the butler for wanting to go home. Why do we have to wait around here, to be slaughtered?"

"We can't stir or move a thing till the police get here," Alice explained. "It's the only thing to do."

"One—two—three—four" pealed from the clock. At the same moment a voice from the radio in the corner intoned solemnly:

"Midnight—and the Gorilla returns to the scene of his latest crime—"

A quick, rapid step sounded on the circular staircase. A series of yells ran around the circle of trembling watchers.

"I want to go home," squealed James.

"Well, gentlemen and lady, have you found any clues yet?" asked a pleasant voice, as the unseen stair climber came into view, disclosing himself as a good-looking young gentleman in his early twenties.

"Wh-ho-ho are you?" stammered William Townsend, tremulously.

"I'm a newspaper reporter. I was at police headquarters when you 'phoned and came right up. Garrity and Mulligan are on their way. They're our two best plainclothes men."

"Hell, what's this!" He examined the warning with professional attention, then cocked his eye at the clock. "Back at midnight, eh? Well, the Gorilla is just five minutes late."

Far away in the silent, death-haunted house boomed a bell. Each looked at the other, tongue-tied and palsied.

"It's the front door bell," quavered the butler. "The Gorilla has kept his word."

"Go see who's there!" commanded young Stevens. "It's your job."

"Not if I was never to hold another as long as I live." James's teeth were chattering.

"We'll all go." Alice led the way in a stampede down the stairs. Marsden bravely flung open the door, and in stalked two individuals with the unmistakable swagger of detectives.

"I'm Mulligan," the taller of the two introduced himself, "and he's Garrity." He pushed a short, thick-set man into the hall. "Now then, what clues have you?"

"I want to go home!" begged the butler. "Oh, Mr. Detective, please let me get out of this place."

"Not on your life!" growled Garrity. "Any one of you may be the murderer. You're all under suspicion." He glared around the circle of white scared faces. Then, charging them not to move, stamped upstairs to the scene of the crime followed by Mulligan. A few moments later he was back, triumphantly brandishing an envelope.

"My father's handwriting!" Alice ran forward. "And addressed to me."

"His last will and testament, probably," Garrity squinted at it. "We found it in the secret wall safe. It takes a detective to uncover clues."

"Open that envelope and you'll have the name of your father's murderer," Mulligan predicted. Alice's shaking fingers drew out the letter.

SNAP! Every light in the room was suddenly extinguished.

"Heaven help us!" shrilled the cook.

"I want to go home!" yapped the butler. "It's that Gorilla back to finish the job."

Stevens found the switch and flooded the room once more with light.

"It's gone!" shrieked Alice Townsend, staring wild-eyed at the empty envelope. "Some one has stolen the letter."

Garrity whirled around to scan each person belligerently.

"Find the person who stole that damning piece of evidence, and you'll have the murderer," he shouted. "He's here in our midst. Let no one leave this room. Garrity, help me search them all."

In the confusion that followed, every one was too fearful of suspicion being cast upon himself to notice a lean, white hand that emerged from the shadows and slipped a piece of note paper inside the leaves of Ridpath's History on the library table.

The results of the search were nil. Garrity and Mulligan shook their heads despairingly.

"Go to your rooms, each of you," ordered the latter. We'll go through things thoroughly and find the clues. There are always bound to be clues somewhere."

"You will never catch the Gorilla," jeered a mocking voice. Garrity rushed to the radio attachment, similar to the one in the cupola above. "The criminal is broadcasting his crimes," ejaculated Mulligan. "Can you beat that for nerve."

"I want to go home," entreated James.

"If we've got to spend the night in solitary confinement," complained Stevens, "I'm going to take a book to read. "He advanced toward the table but before he could make a selection from the row in the rack, William Townsend had hastily snatched up the nearest volume.

"I'll take one, too," said Marsden, helping himself to another, before Stevens could make a choice. And so the party broke up.

Not half an hour later a feeble cry from William Townsend's room brought the household on the run to his door. Only a horrible groan answered Marsden's knock. He thrust his should against the door. It gave way, revealing the second victim of the Gorilla's fiendishness. William Townsend lay outstretched on the bed, the now familiar finger marks on his withered throat. Clutched in his right hand was the letter he had apparently extracted from Redpath's History. Garrity fell upon it and read aloud:

"My darling daughter—I am trapped. There is no hope of escape. My assassin is not a man but—"

"Where's the other half of this sheet of paper?" roared the detective. "The Gorilla strangled William Townsend in order to get it. There was a reason. That missing portion is a clue. I told you, there are always clues."

But no one was listening to him. Every eye was fixed in fearful fascination upon a great shaggy form that was slowly descending by a rope, stretched outside the window, which overlooked the landwide side of the estate.

"The Gorilla!" screamed Alice and fainted dead away.

Garrity and Mulligan were undoubtedly stupid, but they were not cowards. With drawn revolvers they rushed to the outside door to head off the hairy monster as he neared the ground. The group inside waited with terror. Instead of pistol shots they heard a fusillade of oaths.

Then Garrity came clumping back, disgusted and wrathful.

"It wasn't no gorilla," he exploded. "It was that fool butler, in a fur-lined overcoat, letting himself out of the house with a sheet. He wanted to go home. I've chained him up this time. No one is going to leave this dump until the murderer is found."

"The Gorilla will never be found," came the sepulchral tones from the radio. "Abandon your search and leave this place before you all meet the fate of the Townsend brothers."

Garrity leaped upon the radio and wrenched the wooden case apart. Every one in the group started forward thunderstruck. Instead of the usual batteries, a small telephone instrument was disclosed.

"It's the house telephone," gasped Kathie. "It starts in the cellar."

"Whoever has been broadcasting on that radio is right here in this house," cried Mulligan. "Find him and we've got the murderer."

Helter skelter, with drawn guns, the detectives tore down to the basement. They were just in time to catch sight of a bulky silhouette climbing out of the window. Garrity took a flying leap and pulled him back. The man wore a heavy fur overcoat. His face was concealed by a mask. Struggling and hitting out with his heavily gloved hands, he was dragged above to the drawing room. There the detective unmasked him.

"Stevens! Edward Stevens!" came incredulously from Alice's lips. Marsden bent to pick up the crumpled paper the man had dropped. It was the other half of poor Cyrus Townsend's note. "My assassin is not a man," the dead hand had written, "but a fiend in human form, that ingrate whom I took in from the streets and befriended—Edward Stevens."

Garrity snapped the handcuffs over the slinking man's wrists.

"But the Gorilla," inquired Marsden, wonderingly. "What became of the Gorilla?"

"Holy saints!" screamed Kathie, pointing to the window. They all turned to look with crawling scalps and congealed blood at a horrible apparition standing on the window sill—the largest gorilla any of them had ever seen. An instant only it leered at them, then began climbing along the ivy-covered wall toward the roof. But before their fright had had time to abate, an irate Italian laborer burst into the house.

"My monk! Give me backa my monk." He shook his fist in the face of the bemanacled criminal. "You rent him only until tonight. You not keepa him. He my leetle pet."

Hearing his master's voice, the great clumsy simian came clambering back down the ivy, lunged into the room and put his paws affectionately around the Italian.

"He nicea monk," grinned the fellow. "Harmless as a kitten. No more I renta heem out."

The Italian and the gorilla disappeared into the night, leaving Garrity busy with the inspection of Stevens's fur gloves.

"That's how he done the murders." Garrity held up the great, fuzzy fingers. "He'd send the gorilla to the vicinity as a scare and a blind. Then, with these fur gloves on he'd strangle his victims."

A low moan from a chest in the corner of the room interrupted his discourse. Every one rushed to open it. Inside lay William Townsend.

"He didn't quite finish me," he said sitting up, rubbing his throat, "but before I could come to, that gorilla jumped in through the window, lifted me off the bed and dumped me in here. I was so scared I must have fainted."

Marsden and Alice helped him out of the chest, telling him what had happened.

"Thank God you are safe, Uncle William." Alice kissed him tenderly. "Robert and I will need your blessing, as the surviving member of the family, because we're going to be married. It will do dear father's memory no good to postpone the wedding. Indeed, if he knows now how his trust in Edward Stevens was misplaced, I feel sure it is just what he would wish."

Garrity and Mulligan, about to lead off their prisoner, gave a backward look at the young couple.

"I seen it coming," wagged Garrity. "Just by the way she clung to that fellow all through it, I knew how the land lay. A good detective can always find clues."

Moving Picture Stories is on sale at all newsstands. If your local dealer is sold out, send ten cents to Circulation Department, Moving Picture Stories, 112 West 44th Street, New York City, for current or back issues.

Bibliography

Anderson, Robert G. *Faces, Forms, Films: The Artistry of Lon Chaney*. South Brunswick, N.J.: A. S. Barnes, 1971.

Borst, Ronald V., et al. *Graven Images: The Best of Horror, Fantasy, and Science-Fiction Film Art from the Collection of Ronald V. Borst*. New York: Grove Press, 1992.

Brunas, Michael, John Brunas, and Tom Weaver. *Universal Horrors: The Studio's Classic Films, 1931–1946*. Jefferson, N.C.: McFarland, 1990.

Davis, Arnie. *Photoplay Editions and Other Movie Tie-In Books: The Golden Years 1912–1969*. East Waterboro, Me.: Mainely Books, 2002.

Everson, William K. *The Detective in Film*. Secaucus, N.J.: Citadel Press, 1972.

Hanke, Ken. *Charlie Chan at the Movies: History, Filmography and Criticism*. Jefferson, N.C.: McFarland, 1989.

Hardy, Phil (ed.). *The Encyclopedia of Horror Movies*. New York: Harper & Row, 1986.

Harmon, Jim. *Radio Mystery and Adventure and Its Appearance in Film, Television and Other Media*. Jefferson, N.C.: McFarland, 1992.

Johnson, Tom, and Deborah Del Vecchio. *Hammer Films: An Exhaustive Filmography*. Jefferson, N.C.: McFarland, 1996.

Kinnard, Roy. *Horror in Silent Films: A Filmography, 1896–1929*. Jefferson, N.C.: McFarland, 1995.

____. *Science Fiction Serials*. Jefferson, N.C.: McFarland, 1998.

Kohl, Leonard J. *Sinister Serials of Boris Karloff, Bela Lugosi, and Lon Chaney, Jr.* Baltimore: Midnight Marquee Press, 2000.

Mank, Gregory William. *Hollywood Cauldron: Thirteen Horror Films from the Genre's Golden Age*. Jefferson, N.C.: McFarland, 1994.

Miller, Jeffrey S. *The Horror Spoofs of Abbott and Costello*. Jefferson, N.C.: McFarland, 2000.

Miller, Mark A. *Christopher Lee and Peter Cushing and Horror Cinema: A Filmography of Their 22 Collaborations*. Jefferson, N.C.: McFarland, 1995.

Miller, Rick. *Photoplay Editions: A Collector's Guide*. Jefferson, N.C.: McFarland, 2002.

Petaja, Emil. *Photoplay Edition*. San Francisco, Calif.: SISU Publishers, 1975.

Pettigrew, Neil. *The Stop-Motion Filmography*. Jefferson, N.C.: McFarland, 1999.

Pitts, Michael R. *Famous Movie Detectives*. Metuchen, N.J.: Scarecrow Press, 1979.

Senn, Bryan. *Golden Horrors: An Illustrated Critical Filmography, 1931-1939*. Jefferson, N.C.: McFarland, 1996.

Smith, Gary A. *Uneasy Dreams: The Golden Age of British Horror Films, 1956-1976*. Jefferson, N.C.: McFarland, 2000.

Soister, John T. *Of Gods and Monsters: A Critical Guide to Universal Studios' Science Fiction, Horror and Mystery Films, 1929-1939*. Jefferson, N.C.: McFarland, 1999.

Stanley, John. *Revenge of the Creature Features Movie Guide*. 3rd rev. ed. Pacifica, Calif.: Creatures at Large Press, 1988.

Turner, George E., and Michael H. Price. *Forgotten Horrors: The Definitive Edition*. Baltimore: Midnight Marquee Press, 1999.

Wadle, Moe. *The Movie Tie-In Book: A Collector's Guide to Paperback Movie Editions*. Coralville, Iowa: Nostalgia Books, 1994.

Weaver, Tom. *Poverty Row HORRORS!* Jefferson, N.C.: McFarland, 1993.

Weldon, Michael. *The Psychotronic Encyclopedia of Film*. New York: Ballantine Books, 1983.

Williams, Richard. *Readers Library*. 2nd ed., rev. Dragonby, Scunthorpe, North Lincolnshire, England: Dragonby Press, 2000.

Willis, Donald C. *Horror and Science Fiction Films: A Checklist*. Metuchen, N.J.: Scarecrow Press, 1972.

_____. *Horror and Science Fiction Films II*. Metuchen, N.J.: Scarecrow Press, 1982.

_____. *Horror and Science Fiction Films III*. Metuchen, N.J.: Scarecrow Press, 1984.

Young, R. G. *The Encyclopedia of Fantastic Film: Ali Baba to Zombies*. New York: Applause, 2000.

Index

Film titles listed alphabetically in the Catalog, and not also mentioned in the Preface or Introduction, are omitted here. The titles of magazine stories presented in quotation marks in the text are indexed here under their corresponding film titles, in italics.

169